OPERATION WEREWOLF

THE COMPLETE ZINES VOL. 1

THIS VOLUME INCLUDES:

QUIT YOUR JOB. START A FIGHT. PROVE YOU'RE ALIVE. IF YOU DON'T CLAIM YOUR HUMANITY YOU WILL BECOME A STATISTIC.

YOU HAVE BEEN WARNED

Operation VVerewolf

Basic Operations Manual

OPERATION WEREWOLF

I'M JUST HERE FOR THE VIOLENCE 92!

BASIC OPERATIONS MANUAL

WORDS: PAUL WAGGENER/LAYOUT: FRANCISCO ALBANESE

Part I: Our Mission

What is Operation Werewolf?

Mixing together equal parts fight club, strength regimen, motorcycle club and esoteric order, Operation Werewolf is more than the sum of its parts. It is not an organization, but an organism - living and breathing by its tenets and watchwords, "Iron and Blood." It is an affiliation of strength - Wolves among men who recognize one another by the three fingered salute and by the black flag that is their shirt, tank top or battle jacket that reads "Operation Werewolf." These men and women have chosen to gather under this banner because it calls out to their primal natures, that fiery blood that sets them apart from the hopeless grey masses that wander this rock devoid of purpose or joy.

Operatives can be found in countries across the world, dripping sweat on the floor of their spartan-style garage weight room, leaving blood on the dirt in the backyard boxing ring, or bringing their feral competitive style to powerlifting meets, MMA events, bars, back alleys and the savage streets of crumbling cities. They are not products of their environment- instead they change the landscape and environment around them, forgers of destiny, architects of their own becoming. They make the flesh strong, knowing that it is the only fit conveyance for a strong mind and an iron will- theirs is a mindset that accepts no weakness.

Some are solitary practitioners, performing the rituals of life and death amongst the ruins of modern civilization, lone wolves howling songs of destruction and new growth in the woods that encroach on the edges of the rotting Empire, waiting for the fall. Others have made it their mission to seek each other out, forming militaristic divisions, chapters led by their strongest member, creating a war-band that seeks to carve its own myth, to create its own saga of power and might- men and women challenging each other to strive ever higher.

It is not a political statement, but a bloody fist shaken in the face of all institutions of control- a furious bite to the hands that seek to leash or enslave. It is not right or left, but free of these shackles of modern dualistic thinking- it operates under the assumption that the Kings of this world have become so through the forked tongue of finance and fear, and it rejects their offerings. The warriors who make up Operation Werewolf know that the true heroes are those who are self-made, physically and mentally strong, free thinkers and free doers who are both untamed and unrepentant.

Operation Werewolf is a lifestyle, one of constant self-overcoming and hardship. You operatives know that today's effort is tomorrow's reward, and that one must always strive to outdo themselves- each day must be lived as though it is Ragnarok, each hour the last one of our lives.

So make of your bodies a temple, of your will a weapon, of your mind a smokeless fire that reduces this world's lies into ashes. Iron and Blood! 92/XCII

Part II: The Operative

An OPERATIVE is one who has either adopted or found himself already in agreement with the philosophies of OPWW in his daily life, and is living in accordance with the ideas of physical, mental and spiritual strength put forward both in the official transmissions, as well as his own Division, if applicable (see part III.)

We differentiate between an ALLY and an Operative thusly:

An Ally is one who is supporting the Operation from the outside, someone who agrees with what the Operation stands for, but has no interest in further association, formation, participation etc. Often the Ally makes himself useful by sharing propaganda, supporting the war effort through donation, purchase of equipment and so on.

An Operative is one who is directly participating in the Operation from within, representing it through the use of backpatch or other war-gear, attending national and regional events, seeking or attaining membership in a Division, or creating his own. The Operative makes up the backbone of the greater work we are looking to accomplish, and most will fall within this classification. He is considered an ACTIVE UNIT only as long as he makes himself available as such.

A KOMMANDANT is one who has succesfully formed his own DIVISION and is maintaining its upkeep through regular meet-up and event planning. This is an elected position within the Division, and is subject to change at the decision of the majority of Operatives. The Kommandant is the main point of contact for the Division and is expected to represent it at regional and national events, as well as to make himself available for communication with WEREWOLF COMMAND.

The IRON FIST is an elite unit within the greater framework of the Operation. He is one who has exemplified the tenets and principles of OPWW, a specimen both mentally and physically. A member of I.F. adheres to a higher standard of discipline, training and schedule than either the Operative or Kommandant, and induction into this order should be the goal of every Operative who desires the highest level of involvement within the Operation.

WEREWOLF COMMAND is the classification of the founding individual behind Operation Werewolf.

Part III: The Division

A Division is formed based around the following parameters: There are 3 or more individuals in one region desirous of forming a Division. Those individuals have decided who will be the Kommandant of their Division. A Division name has been chosen, and all this information submitted to Werewolf Command.

Once approved, a Division can begin its operations within its region. If there is an existing Division within the area already, it is considered the dominant Division, and should be contacted before forming another - there should be no reason to form more Divisions within a region, and Operatives should seek instead to simply join the existing one. Division may have their own rules for attaining membership and so on, and should be respected by prospective members.

If there are concerns regarding leadership within a Division, members should discuss, and vote on a new Kommandant.

Divisions operations within a region are highly dependent on their members and individual goals, but should certainly include strength training, martial training, monthly events, feasting, fighting, and general comradery. The overall goal of any Division is to foster strength in its members, and to pressure them through peer grouping to attain greater levels of individual glory.

Each Division will have its own symbols, rituals, and style, and this is encouraged. Nearby Divisions are encouraged to reach out to others to host events and competitions, skill trade and so on.

A Kommandant's job is to ensure regular participation in all events from all members, to organize the events and meet-ups on a regular basis, and to aid the members of his Division become stronger, more skilled, more heroic. If he is not fulfilling this function, or if there are others more suited, he should step down and allow those who are more capable to run the Division.

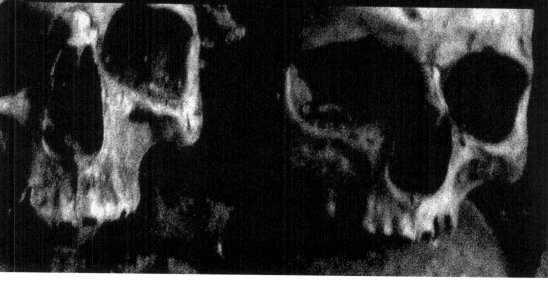

Part IV: A Note On Symbolism and Terminology

If you find yourself in any way put off or offended by the symbolism and terminology of this endeavor, you are more than likely too malleable and influenced by the current accepted narrative to be of any use in this Operation.

Our use of the symbols of our European forebears is neither accidental nor for "shock value" or even to align ourselves with those deluded fantasists that make up most of the current "right." We have no interest in association with individuals who wear their idiocy on their sleeve.

Symbols associated with thousands of years of power have only grown stronger through their ability to create immediate aversion in the hearts of those who cannot grasp that power, or how that power can be turned to serve its master. These symbols are older than any modern civilization and course with STRENGTH and MEANING for those unafraid to delve into their use.

For those who believe that the use of the swastika, the wolf-rune, the black sun, and so forth, automatically force one into a "political" agenda, we will not abase ourselves by attempting to argue against that kind of stupidity. Those individuals who introduced the use of the aforementioned symbols into the aesthetic and ritual of the Third Reich were aware of their form and function long before that failed regime ever came to power.

OUR GOALS AND METHODS ARE ABOVE THE MERE POLITICAL. WE STRIVE FOR SOMETHING GREATER.

Part V: Further Involvement

Many questions arise in the uneducated mind. If you have inquiries or questions, the first place to look should be in the COMPLETE TRANSMISSIONS, available from Werewolf Command. This very brief booklet is designed to answer most of the basic ones, but is obviously not an all-encompassing look at the topic. Before asking questions, exhaust your resources first.

Those who start by asking many questions that could be easily answered for themselves display from the beginning a mind and character that is more than likely unfit or unprepared for the Operation.

Operation Werewolf

no I/IV

To all Operatives around the world:
We have but one life to live.
Arise, and Conquer.

Stick to your guns and let the black flag fly. No quarter asked or given.

REWILD YOUR LIFE

ISSUE #1

So bleak is the picture... that the bulldozer and not the atomic bomb may turn out to be the most destructive invention of the 20th century...

–Philip Shabecoff, New York Times Magazine, 4 June 1978

1: THE GREAT DEPRESSION

The increase in mass urbanization worldwide has provoked studies that are proving conclusively a corresponding increase in psychosis, depression and general mental illness. This occurs because of the combining effects of poverty, crime, drug use, overcrowding, pollution, dissolving family structure, and all the anxieties and negative properties that these things have on the individual. Urbanization and so-called "human progress" has really been a long and systemized domestication process, so that you, the individual, would shut your mouth and go along with the program in order to make a small percentage of the world's population wealthy while your spirit and dreams atrophy and die along with the green world around you.

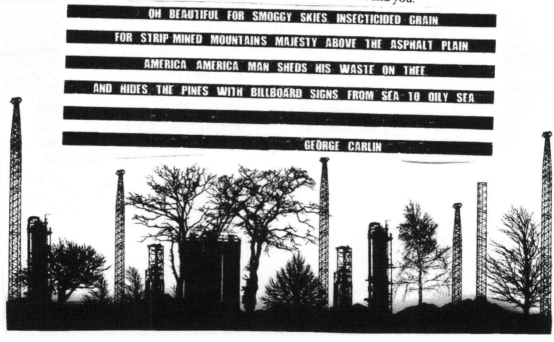

OH BEAUTIFUL FOR SMOGGY SKIES INSECTICIDED GRAIN

FOR STRIP-MINED MOUNTAINS MAJESTY ABOVE THE ASPHALT PLAIN

AMERICA AMERICA MAN SHEDS HIS WASTE ON THEE

AND HIDES THE PINES WITH BILLBOARD SIGNS FROM SEA TO OILY SEA

GEORGE CARLIN

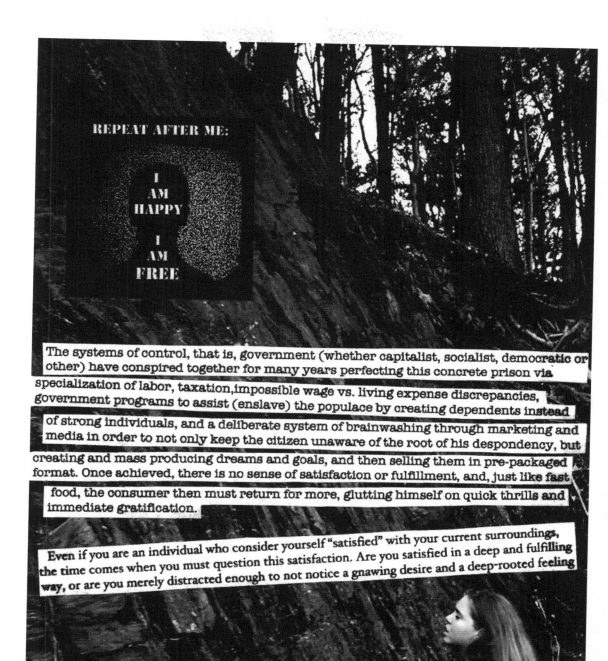

REPEAT AFTER ME:

I
AM
HAPPY

I
AM
FREE

The systems of control, that is, government (whether capitalist, socialist, democratic or other) have conspired together for many years perfecting this concrete prison via specialization of labor, taxation, impossible wage vs. living expense discrepancies, government programs to assist (enslave) the populace by creating dependents instead of strong individuals, and a deliberate system of brainwashing through marketing and media in order to not only keep the citizen unaware of the root of his despondency, but creating and mass producing dreams and goals, and then selling them in pre-packaged format. Once achieved, there is no sense of satisfaction or fulfillment, and, just like fast food, the consumer then must return for more, glutting himself on quick thrills and immediate gratification.

Even if you are an individual who consider yourself "satisfied" with your current surroundings, the time comes when you must question this satisfaction. Are you satisfied in a deep and fulfilling way, or are you merely distracted enough to not notice a gnawing desire and a deep-rooted feeling

THAT YOU DESERVE SOMETHING BETTER?

If you are like most folks here in the wonderful USA, you work for roughly 40 hours or more in a week in order to make a borderline poverty wage, you rent an abode to shelter in because you cannot afford to own (and even if you could, taxes are in place to make sure you never stop paying...even for the things you supposedly own!), you eat unhealthy and/or chemically and genetically modified foods, exercise less than you ought to and watch TV and use the internet for drastically more time in a week than you spend reading, creating art or spending time in what could be loosely termed as "natural" surroundings.

BECAUSE OF THIS, YOU ARE ENSLAVED. YOU ARE A COG IN THE WHEEL OF A GREAT MACHINE, WHETHER YOU LIKE IT OR NOT, AND THAT MACHINE WILL ATTEMPT TO CRUSH YOU IF YOU DEVIATE FROM THE GRANDSCHEME-
YOU ARE TRAPPED IN PLACE AS A DRONE, FIT ONLY TO WORK AND CONSUME AND SLEEP AND WORK AND CONSUME
AD NAUSEUM,
AD INFINITUM,
UNTIL YOU DIE...

Or are you?

"Thousands of tired, nerve-shaken, over-civilized people are beginning to find out that going to the mountain is going home; that wildness is necessity; that mountain parks and reservations are useful

not only as fountains of timber and irrigating rivers, but as fountains of life."

—John Muir

JOHN MUIR SEATED IN YOSEMITE 1907

2: THE GREAT ESCAPE

The essential tool to escaping this pervading grey death of banality and drudgery is one you already have at your disposal, but may have placed deep down in your psyche where it couldn't bother you, an adult, with its childish and silly voice. That voice is the lust for adventure and the awe and wonder we have for life itself- we have silenced this voice, and been told to silence it ever since we were "old enough to know better," or were told enough times to "grow up," when we suggested something spontaneous and wild.

But in order to break down the walls of our own perception, dulled and weakened by this cage of distraction, we must become elite commandos, focusing and honing our skills with the weapons of thought and action- making precise and ruinous strikes against complacency, despair and control. How do we make these strikes? We rediscover the ways and means to a fulfilling, adventurous and heroic lifestyle- because before we can take meaningful action in this unconventional war, we need to know what those actions are. In short, we must embark on a quest of discovery to find out what truly fulfills us. Knowing the answer to this question is one of the most damaging things that can be done to the established system, because for so long, they have been telling you what you need and want! Once you grasp the false nature of their offers, it falls on you to make your own dreams-

DO YOU HAVE WHAT IT TAKES? Good.

TO START ON THIS JOURNEY, ALL WE NEED IS AN ADVENTUROUS SPIRIT WILLING
TO EXPLORE, LITERALLY AND FIGURATIVELY.
OPEN YOUR EYES AND TAKE A LOOK AROUND: AT YOUR LIFE, RELATIONSHIPS,
ACTIVITIES, SURROUNDINGS, WORK ROUTINE (YOU STILL HAVE ONE OF THOSE?!),
THE WHOLE NINE YARDS.
WHAT ASPECTS DO YOU LOVE?
WHICH DO YOU DESPISE?
WHAT ARE TEN THINGS YOU'VE ALWAYS WANTED TO DO, BUT NEVER DID,
FOR WHATEVER REASON?
GIVE 'EM A SHOT- BECAUSE YOU, AND NO ONE ELSE, ARE RESPONSIBLE FOR
THE SHAPING OF YOUR LIFE AND HAPPINESS AND FREEDOM.

TO BE A FREEDOM FIGHTER, YOU HAVE TO START AT HOME BASE:
WITH YOURSELF.

SO REPLACE ALL THOSE GREY AND ARTIFICIAL IDEAS AND GOALS AND PRINCIPLES
WITH A WILD, UNCHAINED DRIVE TO LIVE SPONTANEOUSLY-
TRY NEW THINGS, MASTER NEW SKILLS,
START A REAL WAR AGAINST THE OBSTACLES LIMITING YOUR ABILITY TO
EXPRESS AND MASTER YOUR OWN DESTINY!

"We're not on our journey to save the world but to save ourselves.
But in doing that, you save the world. The influence of a vital
person vitalizes."   - Joseph Campbell

Start thinking about alternate ways to live, to survive, to enjoy yourself. Question your preconceived notions about the way these things are done. If you live within the confines of the city, destroy it's confining ability by realizing its nature as your playground, your refrigerator and food supply, your wild domain.

Imagine that every time you step out your front door, you embark on an adventure to somewhere you've never been, or come up with new ways to get to the places you've already explored. Take friends on "nature hikes" through the urban jungle, get yourselves lost, climb the highest buildings, plumb the depths of the drainage tunnels, find interesting buildings and go inside. Limiting your freedom of mobility, and imagination, is one of the cruelest tools of the civilized world.

Don't stand for it.

Instead of walking out that door to begin your soul-crushing work week, take a detour to freedom. Think up different ways to feed yourself, or clothe yourself, or entertain yourself. Try getting your food out of that bakery dumpster, or help yourself to the clothing out of a donation box and get to work on it with paint, needle, thread or whatever.

Make It
Your Own.

Stand out from the crowd as you develop the primitive markings and ceremonial clothing of your own tribe- turn everything around you into a work of art, including the drab city walls.

Incorporating all these ideas together turns your very life into a strange and wonderful work of art itself-

AND THIS IS NO SMALL THING.

NO ONE'S WORDS, OPINIONS OR THOUGHTS SHOULD BE TAKEN AS REPLACEMENT FOR YOUR OWN.

But as you discover your own voice and lest you think yourself alone on this perilous journey into the Wild, here are a few writings, websites and artists that relate to the current issue, just to get you started:

"In Praise of Idleness," by Bertrand Russell-
a wonderful piece in which Mr. Russell attacks the sacred idea that labor is a virtuous enterprise.

"Running on Emptiness," by John Zerzan-
America's most famous anarchist writer discourses on a variety of topics aimed at the soullessness of the modern world.

"Walden," by Henry David Thoreau-
a voyage of self discovery and simple living in the woods.
A quote: "I went to the woods because I wished to live deliberately, to front only the essential facts of life, and see if I could not learn what it had to teach, and not, when I came to die, discover that I had not lived..."

Crimethinc.com-
Plenty of good material here on nearly every topic relating to anarchism.
Also tons of cheap and free swag for the thrifty anarchist!

Metalographerphotography.tumblr:
Artistic/Documentary Photographer whose images are seen throughout this zine.

Grimnir.tumblr:
A collection of essays, videos and photos detailing and documenting a collective of artists, musicians and tribalists in the Central VA area.

Actionsquad.org-
some inspiration for your urban adventures.

Freegan.info-
a website designed to share strategies that reject the current economic structure. Plenty of good info here.

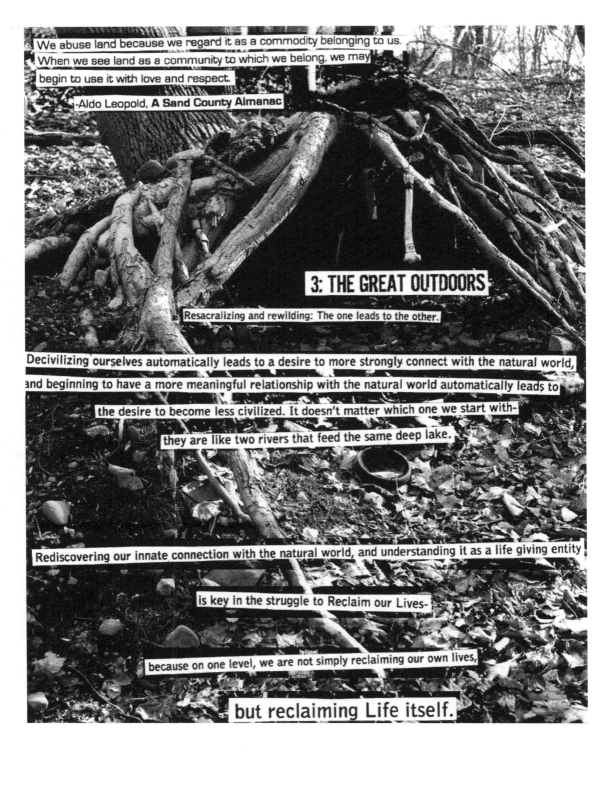

We abuse land because we regard it as a commodity belonging to us. When we see land as a community to which we belong, we may begin to use it with love and respect.

-Aldo Leopold, **A Sand County Almanac**

3: THE GREAT OUTDOORS

Resacralizing and rewilding: The one leads to the other.

Decivilizing ourselves automatically leads to a desire to more strongly connect with the natural world, and beginning to have a more meaningful relationship with the natural world automatically leads to the desire to become less civilized. It doesn't matter which one we start with- they are like two rivers that feed the same deep lake.

Rediscovering our innate connection with the natural world, and understanding it as a life giving entity

is key in the struggle to Reclaim our Lives-

because on one level, we are not simply reclaiming our own lives,

but reclaiming Life itself.

WE ARE IT'S DEFENDERS-

Earth Walkers, Forest Dwellers, Urban Wild Men

and Women,

a myriad of tribes and lone wolves seeking to reawaken that well-spring of vitality and terrible joy that is to be truly **Alive.**

Our awakening comes with the deep rooted **Call of the Wild-** whether we answer it's call by turning the cities into a wilderness, or by abandoning these heaping hulks of concrete and steel in order to return to a disappearing woodland, and fighting for it's preservation with tooth and claw,

our desire is the same: to build a new world and new dreams in the rubble and ashes of the old.

The answers are still unclear as to exactly how this new world will be- but one thing that is certain:

it
will
be

WILD

SOWING THE SEEDS OF COLLAPSE

These technomancers weave their web with neon tracers, their empty power spiraling lifelessly out over the electrical waves, the ocean of hunger. Their sorceries are diversions, each new development designed to sustain your interest longer, to captivate not your imagination but your time- your life. A clever device for storing useless data, or another minor convenience that further atrophies the already weakened muscles of self-reliance in our time.

Their incantations use words like "terabyte", "LCD", "hi-def", "RPM." They ply their trade like high tech gypsies, distracting you with tricks while they steal your children and rob you blind, the echoes of their siren song still ringing. They whisper in the ears of world rulers and their contraptions start wars, prolong wars, end wars, start new wars. Everyone wants to kill for the Next Big Thing. Thousand dollar communication devices have taken over our lives. Digital imaging machines that take 200 shots per second make a picture not worth a thousand words, but rather make a thousand pictures not even worth one word. Life is no longer experienced head-on with a ferocious love. It is reviewed in digital format- each experience merely a pose to later place into the great tentacles of the Internet.

We can escape this grey sickness that has grasped a hold of even the strong, but to do so will require sacrifice: that of our civilization. We as a species have grown pampered and weak, each of us living more comfortably than a thousand kings of antiquity- water, light, heat on command. Food, clothing, gadgetry around every corner for easy consumption. Isolated. Tamed. Controlled. Reliant. Pathetic. Ignorant. Lazy. These are a few of the nicer words that come to mind describing the human condition in present day society. Whether this is because corporate globalization and modern merchant control has dictated this to be our fate, or because we as a people started the snowball effect of ill-advised "progress" and this was its natural outcome is an irrelevant question. All that matters is how we choose to combat this unhealthy, dehumanizing and dominating global situation.

There are more arguments on this front, more words and forums and internet chat rooms and explanations and philosophies and suggested solutions etc. etc. etc. than there are stars in the sky. All of them seem dedicated to whatever the latest buzzword in the modern "anarchist" vocabulary might be, talk upon talk and, unsurprisingly, very little action. This is because the voices on all sides are often of an "all or nothing" slant- one must completely remove oneself from modern society and begin life in a mud hut on Day One, or he must embrace totally the technocratic construct of corporate whoredom and revel in all its might, terror and splendor until his last, smog-filled breath.

The reality is, this "rewilding" is necessary, but must occur on a measured scale of involvement. One cannot simply acquire the skills needed for feral living overnight and move into a hide wikiup the next morning, but nor should s/he succumb to being overwhelmed and give up. There is a natural, more organic method than kicking civilization "cold turkey," that being a slow but steady reintegration and re-education process ultimately leading to a full, well-thought change in lifestyle, worldview and practical living.

It cannot be expected that we close a gap of generation upon generation in a single day, but it can be expected that we END THIS CYCLE NOW, while we are the current generation- otherwise we leave the same sad legacy to our children as our parents left for us: slavery to the system we helped sustain. This is an obvious and horrendous curse to place on our descendants, something to be remedied before we create new life if possible, or to fight tooth and claw so that the children we already have are not faced with the same shackles with which we have been chained for our whole lives.

Breathe deep the richness of the black earth. Run your hands over rough bark, smooth stone, soft fur and remember. Listen to the ragged call of the vulture, the bellow of the elk, the bark of the feral dog and add your voice to this wild wonder. The warm sun on your face, the cold wind in your hair, the wet rain on your back, the full moon shining down on this living earth. This is all the inspiration needed to lay down the supercomputer, the switch, the gear, the machine- and stride boldly and fearlessly back into the Womb of All

That Lives. The war is on. Sides are already being chosen. Where do you stand, and what are you achieving for your children and theirs?

> "Hail Day, Hail Day's sons
> Hail night and her kin.
> With love, look on us.
> Send to those sitting here victory.
> Hail to you gods, and you, goddesses
> Hail Earth who gives to All.
> Good spells and speech we ask from you,
> And healing hands in this life.
> -"Sigrdrifumal," author's trans.

NO·GOD·BUT·THE
W·I·L·D

6 TRACKS OF FERAL GREEN N' BLACK METAL
FROM THE HEART OF APPALACHIA
COMING DECEMBER 2011
HTTPS://WWW.FACEBOOK.COM/HUNTERSGROUNDOFFICIAL

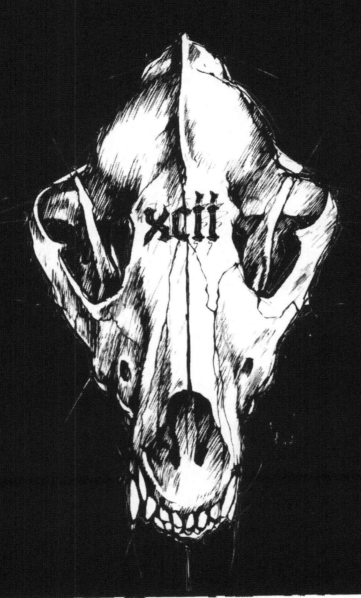

REWILD YOUR LIFE ISSUE #1

REWILD?

What do we mean,

Put simply, a de-civilizing of our minds,

our bodies and our spirits-

an idea that as human beings and creatures

growing on this living earth, we can only

attain by a whole-hearted return to a more

NATURAL relationship with it.

This de-civilizing is meant in a literal fashion,

not as some intellectual analogy-

it is CIVILIZATION

CIVILIZATION

(The word civilization comes from the Latin civilis, meaning civil, related to the Latin civis, meaning citizen, and civitas, meaning city or city-state, referring to its common use as describing that area or person related to so-called "human culture" that is hierarchical, technologically advanced, urbanized, controlled by some form of governing body, etc.)

that is at the very opposite end of the spectrum from words like-

PRIMITIVE

(from Latin primitivus, meaning "first or earliest of its kind," and used here to refer to a basic and uncomplicated approach to life, free of the modern ideas of mediation, governance and complex technologies)

and **WILD**

(from Old English wilde, meaning "in the natural state, uncultivated, undomesticated,")

and **FREE.**

(from O.E. freo "free, exempt from, not in bondage," also "noble; joyful," from P.Gmc. *frijaz)

Now, this is not meant to bore the reader with linguistics, since they are also by their nature corrupt and incapable of expressing true human feeling. Rather, because it is sometimes so

easy to get caught up in the things we find ourselves in revolt **AGAINST**, we lose touch with the things that we are in love with, and seeking to feed within ourselves...

That being said,

our problems with this current world are myriad,

but can be simplified as stemming from three major issues:

OUR MINDS ARE POISONED

from living within a sick society in which self/nature-destroying insanities and horrors are seen as "normal". Where currency and material possessions are the highest (and often the ONLY) attainments one can achieve- this being the thought process that leads to the madness of war for profit, rampant waste, ravage of the environment and most other human atrocity...

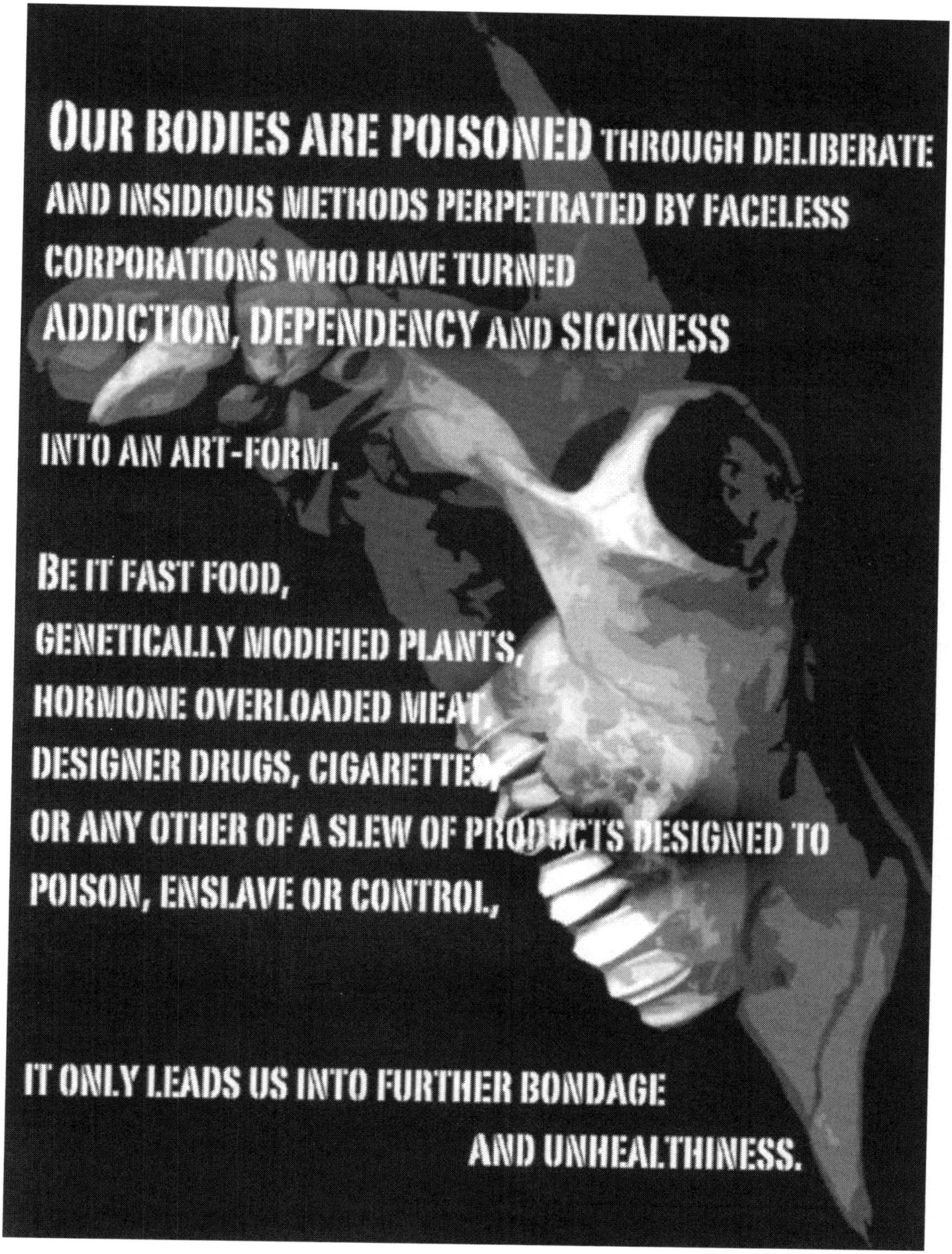

OUR BODIES ARE POISONED THROUGH DELIBERATE AND INSIDIOUS METHODS PERPETRATED BY FACELESS CORPORATIONS WHO HAVE TURNED **ADDICTION, DEPENDENCY** AND **SICKNESS**

INTO AN ART-FORM.

BE IT FAST FOOD,
GENETICALLY MODIFIED PLANTS,
HORMONE OVERLOADED MEAT,
DESIGNER DRUGS, CIGARETTES,
OR ANY OTHER OF A SLEW OF PRODUCTS DESIGNED TO
POISON, ENSLAVE OR CONTROL,

IT ONLY LEADS US INTO FURTHER BONDAGE
AND UNHEALTHINESS.

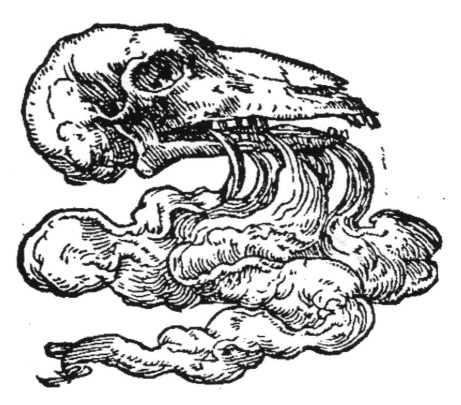

Our spirits have atrophied due to a complete cutting-off of ourselves and our consciousnesses from the wild and wondrous natural world to which we belong. Plant life, animal life, weather events, and so on have become as foreign and frightening to most "civilized" men and women as the idea of life without television or electricity or running water on command. These things have taken over and replaced our relationship with the planet on which we live and the incredible things that we co-inhabit it with— cell-phones, the internet, towering fortresses protecting us from any and all discomfort...

We are rapidly and surely trading away
our humanity, our "creature-ness," to
the ever-quickening current of
technological wonder, convenience,
distraction, trinket. If it cannot be Googled,
it cannot be known. If it cannot be seen on Youtube or
"liked" on Facebook, we are not interested. In fact, our interest in
most things has waned to the attention span of an infant,
casting his gaze about for the next thing to tickle his fancy-
an immobilized sponge,
waiting to soak up the next instant gratification.

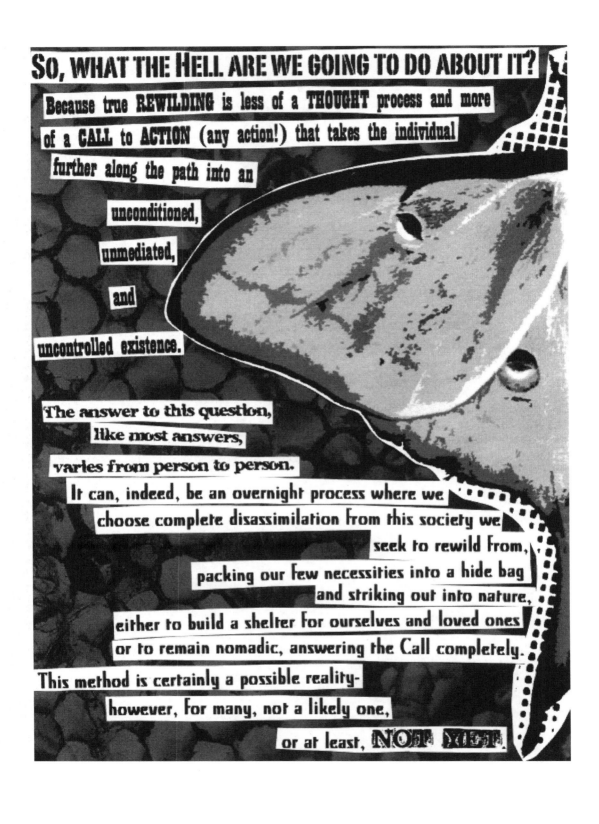

SO, WHAT THE HELL ARE WE GOING TO DO ABOUT IT?

Because true REWILDING is less of a THOUGHT process and more of a CALL to ACTION (any action!) that takes the individual further along the path into an

unconditioned,

unmediated,

and

uncontrolled existence.

The answer to this question,
like most answers,
varies from person to person.
It can, indeed, be an overnight process where we
choose complete disassimilation from this society we
seek to rewild from,
packing our few necessities into a hide bag
and striking out into nature,
either to build a shelter for ourselves and loved ones
or to remain nomadic, answering the Call completely.
This method is certainly a possible reality-
however, for many, not a likely one,
or at least, NOT YET.

'VERILY THE LUST FOR COMFORT
MURDERS THE PASSION OF THE SOUL,
AND THEN WALKS GRINNING IN THE FUNERAL.'
- KALIHL GIBRAN -

For most,
a gentler, more gradual
approach is more desirous.

SO how can we get more WILD,
more FREE without an immediate
haphazard dash into the deep woods?
Here are a few ideas to get you moving—
but any and all things presented here are
only meant as inspiration in order for you
to find your own way into the wilderness.
Only you can live the dreams you have
dreamed...
but get out there and LIVE them!

GET RID OF YOUR SHIT

-ALL OF IT.

TAKE EVERYTHING YOU OWN THAT YOU HAVEN'T USED IN OVER A MONTH (FOR CLOTHES, THIS CULLING RULE GOES FOR ANYTHING YOU HAVEN'T WORN IN MORE THAN TWO WEEKS), AND DO AWAY WITH IT BY ANY MEANS NECESSARY.
GIVE IT TO THRIFT STORES.
TRADE TO FRIENDS.

PUT IT IN A BIG PILE AND **BURN IT.**
WHATEVER.
JUST LOSE IT.
BECAUSE IT IS DEFINITELY DRAGGING ON YOU LIKE A WEIGHT.
FOR SOME PEOPLE, THIS IS A BIG ONE-
FOR SO LONG, WE HAVE BEEN CONDITIONED TO BUY AND TO HOARD,

Can you fit all of the clothes you have now into your biggest pack?

TO KEEP ALL OUR LITTLE
USELESS ITEMS
AND STATUS SYMBOLS
AND WORTHLESS JUNK
THAT THEY'VE TOLD US WE
NEED DEAR TO OUR
GREEDY LITTLE HEARTS.
BUT WE ARE STARTING TO
SEE PAST THEIR ILLUSIONS,
THEIR CONSTANT CALL OF
"BUY IT, BUY IT, BUY IT...TODAY!!!"
AND WE ARE REALIZING THEIR
HUSTLE AND GRIFT
FOR WHAT IT IS.
IT'S LIKE THEY SAY:

SO THE LESS YOU HAVE, THE FREER YOU CAN BE.

"THE THINGS YOU OWN, THEY END UP OWNING YOU."

KILL yOUR TV. -

this is the primary method used to burn your brain, empty your wallet, slow your
mind and subdue your spirit. This statement is not some cute bumper sticker to
show people how "edgy" you are. It is an animalistic impulse to break the manacles
that we put on ourselves every time we hit the power button and sit down on the
couch to "just relax after work." Those pathetic, weak excuses are a thing of the
past. We all know that when we sit down "to relax", we are really being targeted
as mindless consumers, lied to by the so-called "news" networks, placated by
asinine sitcoms and television shows that replace our desires and dreams and
stories with pre-packaged ones- we live out our lives watching actors faking their
way through one hackneyed story-line at a time, all the while wishing,

"Why can't something like that happen to me?"
You have to get off your ass and make the stories happen to you.

TURN OFF YOUR COMPUTER

This is not to say that a computer cannot be a useful tool for communication, the sharing of ideas, the bringing together of people and so on, but the real motivator for this statement is simply that we use these technologies too much- and generally not always for the high-minded examples just mentioned.

If you find yourself spending too much time wasting your time, or if you get off of a two hour session on the internet where you can't even remember what you looked at....it's time for a break.

Go outside and experience something real.

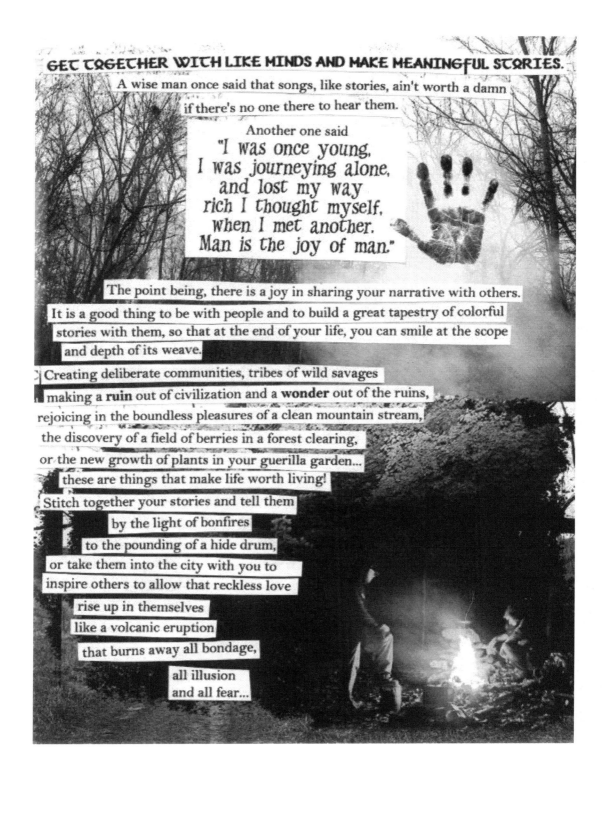

GET TOGETHER WITH LIKE MINDS AND MAKE MEANINGFUL STORIES.

A wise man once said that songs, like stories, ain't worth a damn if there's no one there to hear them.

Another one said
"I was once young,
I was journeying alone,
and lost my way
rich I thought myself,
when I met another.
Man is the joy of man."

The point being, there is a joy in sharing your narrative with others. It is a good thing to be with people and to build a great tapestry of colorful stories with them, so that at the end of your life, you can smile at the scope and depth of its weave.

Creating deliberate communities, tribes of wild savages making a **ruin** out of civilization and a **wonder** out of the ruins, rejoicing in the boundless pleasures of a clean mountain stream, the discovery of a field of berries in a forest clearing, or the new growth of plants in your guerilla garden... these are things that make life worth living! Stitch together your stories and tell them by the light of bonfires to the pounding of a hide drum, or take them into the city with you to inspire others to allow that reckless love rise up in themselves like a volcanic eruption that burns away all bondage, all illusion and all fear...

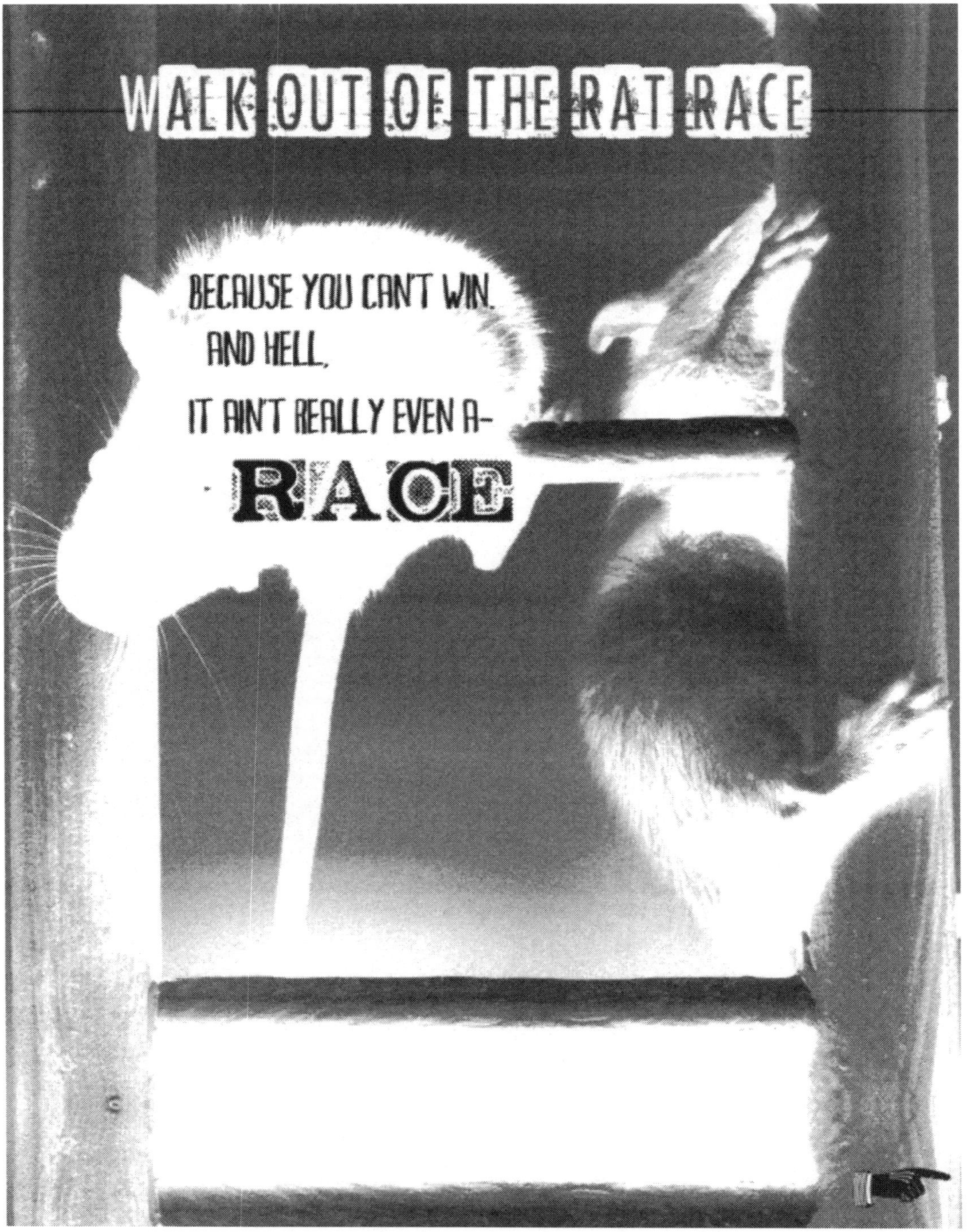

WALK OUT OF THE RAT RACE

BECAUSE YOU CAN'T WIN,
AND HELL,
IT AIN'T REALLY EVEN A-
RACE

IT'S A SCAM.
A LIE.
A MAZE OF RATS,
ALL BELIEVING THERE'S A NICE PIECE OF
CHEESE FOR THEM AT THE END OF THE GREY GRIND,
WHEN ALL THAT AWAITS THEM

IS A MEANINGLESS DEATH.

Is the paycheck at the end of your week really worth the hours of your life you traded away for it? Does each minute of your precious and precarious existence truly have a price tag on it that can be paid in paper currency that you will invariably then barter away for bills or bullshit? The answer of course, is a resounding NO, with a knife directly in the throat of anyone who would tell you that your story, your very existence is relegated to numbers on a finance sheet. At the end of one month, the average US drone will have traded away at least 160 hours of his life for a few bits of paper. If you do the math, this means that somewhere around 22 percent of an individual's life would be spent laboring- made even more frightening if you consider that quite a decent percentage of the other 78 is spent asleep. WHAT FOR? Is this way of living really LIVING? At any cost, discover for yourself new ways to save, or to not spend. New ways to live without trading currency, or if you need currency, new ways to earn it that do not involve punching a time clock and "putting your nose to the grindstone." Freelance with some of your skills, whether they be writing, crafts, art, music, whatever. If you are an experienced landscaper, get out there and bid your own jobs! If you feel you have no skillsets that can make you money, develop some- this is where reading or using the internet can actually benefit you... there are few things that cannot be learned from book, video, or picture, followed by a few hours of practical application. Photography, anything in the repair or maintenance field, the construction field and so on can all be turned into work-for-yourself jobs. Get out there and free yourself from the slavery of the 9 to 5 jive.

A Question Of Technology

"How is it conceivable that all our lauded technological progress--
our very civilization-- is like the axe in the hand of the pathological criminal?"
-Albert Einstein

We here at the REWILDYOURLIFE 'zine spend a lot of time trashing tech.
But obviously, we must spend at least some of our time using technology to type, arrange, photograph and print
the humble pages you are holding in your grubby hands right now.

Is this hypocritical?

Are we just talking the talk and not walking the walk?

Well, yes and no.

The human experience is certainly one of contradictions, failed attempts, minor victories, backsliding, re-application
and progress in increments to where we wish ourselves to be.
We are in no way at that place yet, and as such, we are certainly not yet as free or as wild as we'd like to be.
But we are working on it.
That work comes with the realization that as people raised within this construct,
it is difficult to simply walk away from it.
Some of this can resolve itself by simply trying to find a more **balanced** relationship with the technology we do use,
and limiting its overall use in our lives.

Freeing ourselves from our infatuation/addiction begins with breaking its hold over every aspect of our existence-
leaving our phones off or at home, alotting ourselves a pre-set amount of time using the computer each week,
canceling our cable subscriptions and so on.

None of us have the perfect solution

but we can take hope in each of these little victories due to the knowledge that they will add up-
and if we can replace our time spent using these mediating and often harmful technologies with time in simple silence,
communion with nature,
or face-to-face interaction with real human beings,

then we are certainly moving in the right direction....

WHAT TO DO WITH ALL YOUR NEW FREE TIME (AND SPACE)

Start a garden—
in your yard, in the woods, in the city. Or familiarize with your local flora and fauna and use the whole damn bio region as your garden. Find a place in your urban playground— a rooftop, abandoned parking lot, back alley, or park and make it your own personal growing space. Drag planters in, grow dwarf fruit trees, graft onto existing trees, hang your own totems and power objects from them.

Make an ugly and forgotten place beautiful and productive again— shatter the asphalt and aid the Green in its reclamation of the Grey.

Pick up a new skillset-

learn how to skin and tan roadkill and make bags, clothes, or art from it. Give that dead bird on the roadside a more proud afterlife by using its claws for earrings or necklaces. Deer hooves strung together make good rattles for your young one or your musical endeavors. Pick up an instrument, a paintbrush or a tool and learn how to use it to make your life more interesting and full. Share your newly found abilities with friends and learn theirs. What animal made those tracks by the river?

Work to understand cloud formations, poison plants, entheogens, bird-calls and so on. As you begin to associate these things with their source, you become a part of their world, as you always were, and were always meant to be.

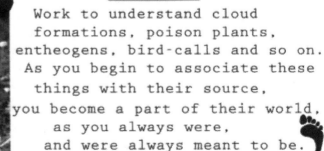

ORGANIZE A SKILL SHARE OR FREE MARKET.

REMEMBER ALL THAT STUFF YOU'RE GOING TO GET RID OF?
GET HOLD OF SOME PEOPLE, FLYER OR USE THE GRAPE-VINE TO ORGANIZE A
TRADE OR FREE MARKET. SET UP SOMEWHERE AND LAY OUT ALL THAT STUFF ON
BLANKETS AND SWAP FOR USEFUL THINGS. OR DISCOVER THE JOY OF GIFT
GIVING TO SOMEONE WHO MIGHT ACTUALLY NEED THE THINGS THAT YOU
CERTAINLY DON'T. THIS IS A THING THAT CAN BE
DONE AS OFTEN AS YOU LIKE,
AND CAN HELP YOU

DISASSOCIATE
FROM THE IDEA
THAT EVERYTHING MUST BE
BOUGHT AND SOLD.

Replace your or your friend's necessaries with handmade or beautified ones. This goes back to the idea of turning your life into ART. All the things you use and wear become an extension of yourself when they are given LIFE and personality through naming, beautifying and personalizing. Each thing becomes a wondrous item in the storyline of your wanderings...

MOST OF ALL,

USE YOUR TIME TO DISCOVER NEW THINGS
ABOUT YOURSELF AND YOUR FRIENDS THAT
YOU DIDN'T EVEN KNOW WERE THERE.
YOUR STRENGTHS AND WEAKNESSES,
YOUR FEARS AND DESIRES
AND WILDEST DREAMS.
ALL THE THINGS THAT MAKE YOU A BEING
OF DEPTH AND EVER-GROWING ROOTS.
NEVER FORGET WHERE YOUR HEART LIES,
AND USE IT AS COMPASS,
THE POINT OF WHICH YOU FOLLOW WITH A
FEROCITY AND SAVAGE WILL THAT NOTHING
CAN TAME OR DOMINATE. STRIKE OUT ON
YOUR PATH EACH DAY WITH A FEROCIOUS
JOY- IT IS THE FIRST STEP ON AN
ADVENTURE THAT WILL LAST YOU THE
REST OF YOUR WILD LIFE.

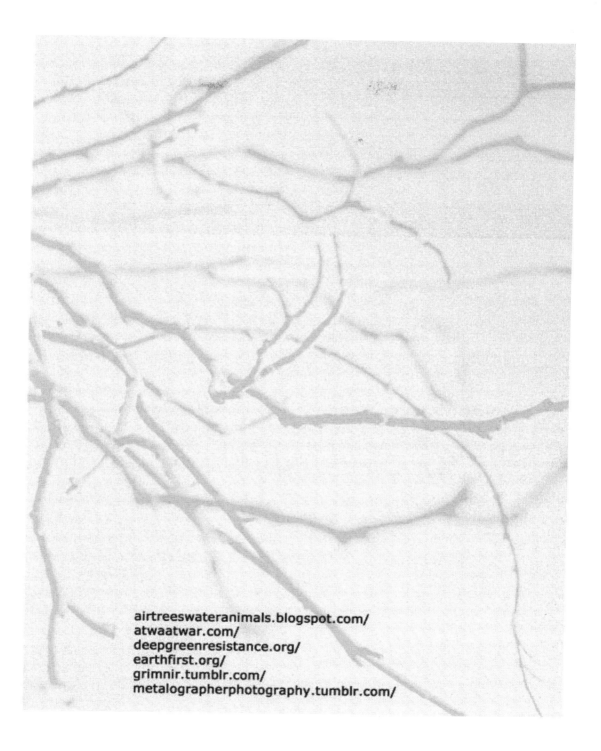

airtreeswateranimals.blogspot.com/
atwaatwar.com/
deepgreenresistance.org/
earthfirst.org/
grimnir.tumblr.com/
metalographerphotography.tumblr.com/

One World Order - you give the foundation of the mind in this -
AIR IS GOD, because without AIR, we do not exist.
So AIR is no. 1 Order.
You don't need a leader, you need intelligence.
You need intelligent mind, One Mind.
One Order to redeem AIR on planet EARTH.

To redeem the AIR, your first and foremost friend is green.
Anything that's green,
like kelp, seaweed, the ocean's contents, the bushes, the grass
and most of all the TREE.

The people are at war with the trees, they're cutting all the trees down.
The TREE is the second form of communication to the intelligent life form.

AIR, TREES, and the WATER is our spirit.
Without the WATER the TREE cannot survive.
So we have to put up our protection for the green, the green things in life.

All the green comes from the sunlight.
The Darwin Theory and all that stupid shit they teach you in school is bunk.
You come from the same place everything else comes from, you come from the SUN.
The SUN puts out all the energy that grows everything,
including me and you, them and they and us.

The World Order does not need a leader.
It just needs established in the intelligence of the mind,
the body of the world and the soul.

The mind, body and soul.
We need to heal the mind.
We need to heal the body and the soul.

We must realize we are no better than the ANIMALS.
We are no better than the zoo.
We've got ourselves locked up in the zoo.

All the people that are so-called living are really dead
and there is no chance to redeem them.
But there is a chance to redeem the dead.
So we are an Order of Dead.
Dead man walking.
I am caveman.
I don't believe I've ever been borned and I don't believe I'll ever die.
Because this body is not me.
I'm just in this body temporarily, traveling through this enclosure.

The mind, the body and the soul is beyond the physical body.
The real Spiritual Soul is in the AIR, in the WATER.
It's in every living thing - bugs, birds, TREES.
There is nothing it's not in.
It's complete and it's the night,
in the stars, the zodiacs and the novas that are going on for ETERNITY is the real eye,
it's the only real, it's the only real, it's the only thing that can be real,
because it circles.

The simplicity of the Order of ATWA is the Order of ALL LIFE and it's just SURVIVAL.

-Charles Manson-

THE OAK: A 300 Word Parable

It was in the most unholy of places—
shattered glass and busted concrete
formed a ruined mosaic floor between
rusting steel beams and metal siding.
Light filtered through holes in the roof,
great gaping spaces
that let in weak rays from the cold sun,
struggling against the great firmament of pollution,
the sky a machine-gun grey,
cheerless and fitful.
But there it was:
between spider webbing cracks
that spelled out ancient runes of new growth,
the tiny Oak found purchase,
little more than a green twig with two small leaves,
rounded at the edges
and speckled with holes from the acidic rainfall.
bravely raising his head
from the safety of the acorn
that bore the precious cargo of his genetic structure,
he found Life
and grasped hold firmly
with his frail roots,
striving against his grim surroundings to Exist.
Round about him were more survivors,
unlikely refugees in this parodic Eden—
there was Mint,
rising up in her little clusters,
shoulder to shoulder and looking quite green in the feeble sunlight;
Tobacco, his wide leaves gently bobbing in a slight breeze
that trailed in from where an old loading door had fallen from its track.
He was neighbored by a small bevy of savory herbs, all enjoying his company.
On the other side of the Oak,
where concrete stairs ran upward to another little landing with more plant boxes,
cobbled together from old palettes, stood Tomato, Squash and a good number of other Edibles,
while several tall young Corn plants raised their slender bodies toward the light,
a few tufts of silk just showing here and there. Datura Stramonium blossomed prettily wherever
she pleased,, white and purple trumpets still closed, awaiting the fall of dusk, her seduction time.
All these and more were present, but Oak was the center of attention, there in the middle of the
Sacred Garden, for he was the Last of His Kind. The final survivor of his age-old people,
still hearing the whisper of his ancestors on the Wind of Time.
His existence was precious but precarious,
withstanding the onslaught of Death, Rage and Ruin.

~by Paul Waggener~

OPERATION WEREWOLF

XCII

long live death!

What you are looking at now is the first issue of Iron and Blood, the official 'zine of Operation Werewolf. This file can be printed out for your own use or to give to friends, leave at the gym, use as a paper target at the range, whatever. As it represents a large time expenditure on my part, each issue will be downloadable at a small charge- if others are interested in obtaining a copy, it would be appreciated if they were sent through the appropriate channels. If you are going to pirate it, at least do it in its full form and make sure it goes to the right people!

Operation Werewolf began as an expansion project to a little movement called the Centurion Method, a primal workout system and philosophy that I had become involved with during its developmental stages a few years back. Unfortunately, it never really got past that stage, as its original creator saw fit to relegate it to the scrap heap and move on to other (I won't say better) things.

Even during that early phase, Operation Werewolf had its own identity, and its own function. It looked to take the savage essence that was the Centurion Method, and do away with some of its less functional trappings, its increasingly political slant, and focus on what I felt was important: the process of creating new heroes in an age devoid of myth.
At its core, this is what Operation Werewolf truly means. To make war on weakness and complacency, first through the act of physical overcoming and the obtaining of strength on a visible, outward level- so that the would-be hero can pass through those Gates of Iron and apply their principles to every area of his being, in a legendary act of Alchemical transformation. We call this process Operation Werewolf.

MIGHT IS RIGHT

This zine is another manifestation of the power and fury of that Operation, and represents a way that those enlisted in this war can not only obtain further inspiration, but submit works of their own in order to communicate with others, and have their battle cry heard far and wide.

xXLUWATUWAXx

Submissions of art and written work can be sent to werewolfcommand@gmail.com and will be used or discarded based on their perceived merit and value to the war effort.

WE ARE LOOKING FOR SUBMISSIONS ON THE TOPICS OF D.I.Y. CULTURE, ESOTERIC WORK AND STUDIES THAT SUPPORT THE GREAT WORK, LIFTING AND STRENGTH TRAINING ARTICLES, LIFESTYLE INSPIRATION, NEWS FROM THE FRONT LINES, DIVISION REPORTS FROM AROUND THE WORLD, AND WHATEVER ELSE YOU THINK MIGHT BE APPRECIATED BY ALL THE GLORIOUS RANKS OF THIS WEREWOLF LEGION.

THOSE WHO ARE LOOKING TO JOIN THE WAR EFFORT BUT ARE UNCERTAIN OF HOW TO PROCEED, OR WHO ARE INTERESTED IN PURSUING TRAINING AND/OR PERSONAL COACHING CAN CONTACT ME AT THE ABOVE LISTED EMAIL FOR CONSULTATION.

I SINCERELY HOPE YOU ENJOY THIS FIRST ISSUE OF "IRON AND BLOOD" 'ZINE. KEEP RISING.

-PAUL WAGGENER, WEREWOLF COMMAND.

If your job makes you FUCKING MISERABLE, and you feel stressed out, unfulfilled, exhausted, beaten down and underpaid.

If all you can seem to manage when you get off for the day is to "put your feet up," turn on the t.v. or netflix and drink a beer, trying to avoid the dread of thinking about doing it ALL. OVER. AGAIN. Tomorrow. and the next day. and the next day. and the next. and...

If you are dissatisified with your physical appearance, looking at your reflection in the mirror with DEFEAT and DESPAIR, unable to take the initiative needed to change yourself.

If you know deep down inside that if the situation called for it, you would be WOEFULLY unprepared to handle yourself capably in a VIOLENT situation.

if you feel that all this is somehow very, very wrong.

YOU ARE CORRECT, AND YOU ARE NOT ALONE.

QUIT MAKING EXCUSES- QUIT YOUR JOB INSTEAD.
BURN YOUR COUCH. THROW YOUR FUCKING T.V. OUT THE WINDOW.

EAT NOTHING BUT LEAN MEAT, VEGETABLES AND CLEAN CARBS.
PICK A SIMPLE WEIGHT TRAINING AND CONDITIONING PROGRAM OFF THE INTERNET
here's a few to get you
AND START RIGHT NOW. STARTED ---->

The "Savage" training blueprint uti-
lizes high frequency training, body-
weight and lighter weight percent-
ages, combined with high intensity
conditioning work to promote lean
muscle, speed, endurance and a low
body fat percentage. Anyone looking
to cut up or maintain a training program that is easier on the joints and
will keep you in fighting form year
round- look no further.

All rest times should be brief 45-60
secs. After Day 6 a rest day can be
taken.

day four-
AM: Fasted 5 minute burpee AMRAP

PM: 100 KB Swings/100 Pull-ups
    5/5 min. rounds Heavy Bag Work

day five-
AM: Fasted jog 1.5 miles
    5 minute burpee AMRAP

PM: Deadlift: 5x5
    Shoulder Press 5x12
    Plate Front Raises 5x20
    Face Pulls/Band pull-aparts 5x12

day six-
AM: 5 20 second sprints
PM: 10 Rounds Heavy Bag

day one:
AM: Fasted jog 1.5 miles
    5 minute burpee AMRAP
PM: Bench Press/Barbell Row 5x12
    Dumbell Flies/Rear Delt Laterals 5x12
    Push Up/Inverted Rows 5 AMRAP

day two:
AM: Fasted 5 minute burpee AMRAP

PM: 100 Kettlebell Swings/100 Pull-ups
    5/5 min. rounds Heavy Bag work

day three-
AM: 5 20 second sprints
    5 minute burpee AMRAP

PM: Barbell Front Squats 5x20
    Stiff Leg Deadlift 5x12
    Barbell Calf Raises 5x20

TRAINING BLUEPRINT
UNIT TYPE: SAVAGE

DAY ONE.
AM: Fasted Walk, 30 minutes
PM: Bench Press 10x3 @ 75-85% of max
    Incline Dumbell Press 4x10
    Cable Crossover 4x15
    Weighted Dips 4xAMRAP
    Tricep Extensions 4x15

*TAKE REST DAYS ONLY WHEN NEEDED.
KEEP REST TO 1.5 MINUTES ON HEAVY
WORK, 45 SECS-1 MINUTE ON
HYPERTROPHY SETS.

DAY TWO.
AM: 5 minute burpee AMRAP, fasted
PM: Squat 10x3 @ 75-85% OF MAX
    Leg Press 3x20
    Stiff Leg Deadlift 3x10
    Glute Ham Raise or Ham Curl 4xAMRAP
    Calf Raises 3 variants, 5 sets each 15-20 rep

DAY THREE.
AM: Fasted Jog, 1.5 miles, with 3 20 second sprints during
PM: Overhead Press 10x3 @ 75-85% max
    Seated DB Press 4x10
    Rear Delt Flies 3x15
    Front to Overhead Plate raises 100 reps

DAY FOUR.
AM: 5 rounds of 20 KB Swings, 20 Burpees.
Deadlifts. Work up to heavy singles at 90% max.
Weighted Chin/Pull-ups 5 sets descending to unweighted AMRAP.
Yates Rows 4x10-15
Single Arm Dumbell Rows 3x20 each side

TRAINING BLUEPRINT
UNIT TYPE: BERSERKER

This routine should be adhered to for those seeking a mixture of
brute strength and devastating conditioning. It mixes traditional
strength training with the best and simplest H.I.T. workouts to
make it both easy to follow and effective as hell. Get strong as
fuck. Stay lean as fuck. (Obviously, as with the other blueprints included here, the Berserker training method is useless without
proper nutrition to back the regimen.)

TRAINING BLUEPRINT
UNIT TYPE: JOTUNN

In order to develop massive
strength, the trainee must move
massive weights, eat massive meals,
and get good amounts of sleep.

These are the three key character-
istics of any good training regimen. For the building of pure,
brute power, there are few routines
better than a simple push-pull.

The Jotunn training split is as
follows:

DAY 1:
(Incline or Flat Bench.) 10 sets of 3 reps at between
75-90% of your 1 rep max. Test your 1RM at the beginning
of each month, and progress accordingly.
(Heavy Yates or Pendlay Rows.) Use care with form and hit 3 sets of progressively heavier
weights in the 6-10 rep range and one "all out" set of As Many Reps As Possible (AMRAP)
(Squat.) Use the same rep and weight range as your Bench Press. A general rule of thumb
for all Jotunn training is to stay at heavy weights, between 1-6 reps per set, for a total
of somewhere around 30 reps spread between all sets.

DAY 2: OFF

DAY 3:
(Overhead Press.) Singles, doubles, triples, at heavy weights, again, using somewhere around
75-90% of maximum weight. Strict press or push press when fatigue sets in.
(Weighted Chins.) Using a weight belt, add resistance to your chin up sets. Everything
heavy, everything difficult. Try to add weight every time you train, even if only a single
pound, or a single rep. This is progressive overload, and it is how you get stronger. Do 5
sets AMRAP, alternating grip each set. Record weights and reps and beat them next time.
(Deadlift.) Progressively heavier weights, working up to a few heavy singles at 90% of your
max. Deadlift is a man-maker, and will put thickness and power into your frame.

DAY 4: OFF

DAY 5:
Same as Day 1. This program has little variance from Bench, OHP, Squat, Deadlift, and for
good reason. It is these main lifts that every program should be built around, whatever
the goal. They are the four pillars of Strength, and combined with rowing and weighted
chins, along with proper diet, will create a powerful and massive build.

DAY 6: OFF.

HERE'S THE THING ABOUT PEOPLE WHO ARE ALWAYS TALKING SHIT:

WHILE YOU'RE OUT THERE
PURSUING YOUR DREAMS,
ACHIEVING YOUR GOALS,
MAKING NEW ONES,
CHALLENGING YOURSELF
SPREADING YOUR INFLUENCE,
BETTERING WHO YOU ARE,
CONQUERING UNKNOWN TERRITORY,
MAKING CONNECTIONS,
INCREASING YOUR VALUE,
HUSTLING HARD,
SUCCEEDING IN YOUR FIELD
AND TAKING NO FUCKING PRISONERS-

ALL THEY'RE DOING...

IS TALKING SHIT.

#OPERATIONWEREWOLF

Traps Against the Modern World

Strong traps are a sure indicator of a powerful physique. Like a thick neck, I don't think I have ever seen a good set of traps on someone who wasn't strong. Unlike a six pack or big arms, which can be seen on the average curl bro in abundance, traps require heavy deadlifting, shrugs, rack pulls, and a plethora of other strength exercises in order to build a hefty slab of muscle across the upper back.
There's nothing wrong with being lean and having a killer set of abs, either- it's just that is more indicative of low body fat and has fuck-all to do with real power.

In this article we will take a look at some of the best ways to develop a mighty set of traps that would be at home in any Frank Frazetta painting and inspire fear in your enemies and lust in women. First thing to think about is frequency and intensity. If you're not hitting the trap with as much ferocity and attention as you do bench day, then you can't expect to walk around with the benefits. You don't deserve traps- you have to work for them. If you are hitting them once a week, try doing direct work twice a week, or even every other day along with abs and calves, or whatever other frequency work you're doing.

SHRUGS- The obvious go-to choice for traps. However, what we really want to do here is mix it up. If you only do heavy shrugs for your traps, try doing bigger sets of lighter weights on one of your trap days. By the same token, if you normally don't go really heavy on shrugs- go as heavy as you can for a lot of sets of few reps.

BARBELL OR KETTLEBELL HIGH PULL- Similar to an upright row, but the focus is on getting the bar or bell as high as humanly possible at the top of the lift, really contracting the hell out of the muscle at the top. For this exercise I prefer lighter weights, and tons of reps.

FRONT PLATE RAISES TO OVERHEAD- Like a normal plate raise, but instead of stopping at eye level with the plate, continue in a smooth motion until the weight is straight overhead. Keep the arms straight throughout the whole movement, and do as many reps as humanly possible at a time, all the way up to 75 or 100 reps with as much weight as you can use while keeping form. Most people should stick to around 25 here so they don't sacrifice form.

REAR DELT FLIES- These can be used last as a finisher for the middle traps, but must be correctly performed so as not to hit the shoulder only. Get at the edge of a bench, and lay down the chest on the knees, keeping your head down and looking at the floor. The dumbells will be behind your heels on the floor. Keeping the arms only slightly bent at the elbow, perform a smooth reverse fly movement and contract the traps hard at the top. Do in high sets with light weight.

Use these exercises to bring your traps up to speed, and perform them in various combinations. The traps can take a beating, so give it to em and grow!

DIVISION

AS WEREWOLF OPERATIVES ACROSS NATIONS COME TOGETHER TO FORM DIVISIONS, AND SOLITARY PRACTITIONERS FLY THE DEATH-WOLF STANDARD TO SHOW THEIR AFFILIATION, THE NEXT STEP IS CONSIDERED: HOW WILL YOUR DIVISION FUNCTION? WHAT WILL IT LOOK LIKE IN PRACTICE, IN FORM, IN TRIBAL MARKING? AFTER ASSEMBLING AT LEAST 3 OPERATIVES AND SUBMITTING THE DIVISION NAME AND LOCALE FOR APPROVAL, WHAT COMES NEXT FOR THE DIVISION LEADER AND THE OTHER OPERATIVES FORMING THIS NEW UNIT?

THE ANSWERS TO THESE QUESTIONS VARY ENTIRELY ON THE DIVISION, BUT ARE IMPORTANT ONES FOR THE FLEDGLING UNIT TO DECIDE UPON. HOW TIGHT THE STRUCTURE OF A GROUP IS FROM THE BEGINNING WILL LARGELY DETERMINE ITS FUNCTION LATER ON DOWN THE ROAD- AN ORGANIZATION THAT BEGINS IN A LOOSE AND MORE ORGANIC FORM WILL MOST LIKELY REMAIN THAT WAY, AS IT IS DIFFICULT TO ADD RIGIDITY TO A STRUCTURE AFTER ITS INCEPTION.

A DIVISION THAT BEGINS IN A MORE ORDERED AND STRUCTURED FASHION WILL OBVIOUSLY HAVE A DIFFERENT LOOK AND FEEL, AND BECAUSE OF THIS, WILL FIND ITSELF FULFILLING A DIFFERENT FUNCTION THAN OTHERS, ALTHOUGH ALL OPERATIVES BEAR THE TOTENWOLF, THERE ARE MYRIAD WAYS A DIVISION CAN MARK ITSELF TO PROMOTE UNIT PRIDE AND A SENSE OF TRIBALISM WITHIN: SPECIFIC COLORS USED, PATCHES, PAINT, OR BY-WORDS IN LINE WITH THE CHOSEN DIVISION NAME: SPECIALTY WITHIN THE LARGER NETWORK OF OPERATIVES BY SKILLSET-

FOR EXAMPLE A DIVISION LED BY SOMEONE WHO INSTRUCTS MUAY THAI IS LIKELY TO HAVE A HEAVIER FOCUS ON TRAINING FOR CONDITIONING AND HAND-TO-HAND THAN ONE LED BY A POWERLIFTER, IN THIS WAY, AN OPERATIVE IN THE FUTURE WILL HAVE CHOICES AVAILABLE TO HIM WHEN HE CONSIDERS WHAT DIVISION APPEALS TO HIM MOST BASED ON ITS FORM AND FUNCTION, AND CAN LOOK TO UNDERGO THE TESTS AND TRIALS REQUIRED BY THAT UNIT IN ORDER TO BECOME A MEMBER.

This leads us to our next question: What will Divisions require of new members, or veteran Operatives who are applying to join their Division?

Will there be a boot camp of sorts, or a "prospecting/probationary" period? Will it be open to any and all to join? Are there specific requirements for this Division that makes it different from others, or more specialized? These issues need to be addressed upon the formation of a new Division and clearly understood by its members before events are put on and things begin to take shape.

Obviously, the emphasis in Operation Werewolf is face-to-face meetings, and the development of Divisions that meet regularly, made up of individuals who want to push and be pushed to higher standards of physical, mental and spiritual performance. Because of this, it is important that Divisions begin holding regularly scheduled events, both on a private and open level. What this looks like, again, will be up to the Division. Private events can be monthly or weekly, but should not be less frequent than every other month at the very least, whether this is a meet-up at a gym, home location, training field, whatever. The activities should cover the physical, mental and spiritual spectrum, with all operatives coming away recharged and better for it.

An example of this would be the operatives meeting at a local gym or the garage gym of a member to lift weights and box or grapple, followed by a meal and group discussion regarding Divisional business. From there, a talk on a what the operatives are doing to push themselves mentally— what books are being read etc. This could be followed by a symbel, a ritual tradition that is incredibly bonding and strengthening.

Those with a deeper interest in ritual or spiritual traditions can begin to develop these organically with the Division— down the road, each Division may have its own highly developed and extremely unique mythos around which these rituals are based. The way forward is the Division— strong individuals are needed to form these Divisions: hard-chargers with a gut full of fire and a firm grasp on the tenets of Operation Werewolf. Leaders of men, illuminated barbarians prepared to undergo the Change— that lycanthropic shift from Man to Wolf symbolized by our Wolf-rune.

These men are berserkers charging towards Truth, gnashing their teeth against the falsehood and weakness of the Kali Yuga, not content to weep and give in to the beast of modernity— but to savagely charge it, leap upon its spear-wounded back and ride it into the ground! In order to re-establish value in this world, we must give worth and life back to those principles which promote strength and fierce joy: physical power, mental sharpness, spiritual depth, brotherhood and sisterhood, tribe, ferocity and laughter at this wondrous thing called Life that pumps through our healthy veins.

Adventure and experience create powerful humans.

Faced alone, they are an enjoyable challenge.

Faced with brothers, they are a true joy for the man who knows the invincibility which tribe can bring.

92!

equalizers-
utilizing improvised
weapons

In the often dangerous world we live in, an intelligent individual will take precautions in order to be sure that he can defend himself. While this can mean anything from training in various martial arts to carrying a handgun, there are times when another strategy must be considered.

We cannot always carry a firearm on our person due to legal constraints, or times where we would rather not carry a weapon to avoid the ever-present eyes of the law. If we are outnumbered, our training in hand to hand combat may not be sufficient to devastate a superior number of attackers. If female, one often needs something to even the odds with a male attacker.

I have never been fond of the idea of a "fair fight," unless one is engaged in competition for its own sake. In a truly violent situation, one must either win or risk death, serious injury, or other dramatic harm to their person-

an asocially violent encounter calls for asocially violent methods. These methods should never be used unless absolutely necessary- when one is certain they are in the right to use deadly force.

Improvised weapons can act as brutal equalizers in just such a situation, and they have the added benefits of not attracting unwanted attention from law enforcement, the ability to carry them anywhere, uses beyond mere weaponry, and the most useful- being better than an unarmed attack. Here are some of what I consider to be the best improvised weapons in my personal arsenal. I have used several of these with successful results in the past, and would recommend that the aware individual find ways to implement their availability in his car, on his person, and wherever else he may find himself in need.

Loose Change. Perhaps one of the stranger sounding items on this list, but effective
nonetheless. Almost everyone usually has this on their person throughout the day, and
it is one of the least harmful seeming objects one can have on their person. If a situation arises, whether or mugging or some other form of rapidly escalating confrontation,
the good rule of thumb is to strike first, strike hard, strike last. In order to facilitate this, a handful of change can be grabbed from the pocket and flung hard in a potential attacker's face. The idea here is not necessarily to cause much damage, but to
create a response. Nearly everyone will flinch when busted in the face by a handful of
nickels, and this reaction can create enough time to launch a devastating assault.

Maglight. Pretty obvious one. Carried on the person (obviously not an everyday carry
for the larger ones, but even a small, belt size maglight can be carried in the fist as
a fist-pack, or the butt can be brought to bear as an effective striking weapon) or in
the car, a full size maglight is an imposing crushing weapon. Usefulness outside a
striker is obvious. Should be part of everyone's vehicle kit, within easy reach by the
center console.

LET A MAN NEVER STIR ON HIS ROAD A STEP WITHOUT HIS WEAPONS OF
WAR; FOR UNSURE IS THE KNOWING WHEN NEED SHALL ARISE OF A
SPEAR ON THE WAY WITHOUT. -HAVAMAL 38

Steel Drinking Bottle. Another great striking weapon, especially the smaller sized ones
with contour for gripping. Stainless steel is unforgiving, and can be carried openly everywhere. Late night jogging companion for the prepared.

Prescription Cane. A prescription for a cane can be obtained relatively easily through
some intelligent planning. With a prescription, a stout piece of hardwood can be kept on
one's person in bars, airports, and anywhere else the need might arise for it. Good reach,
obvious effectiveness.

Titanium Pen. Another easy carry that is allowed anywhere, a titanium pen is virtually
unbreakable and can be used as a stabbing weapon in a serious situation.

Last but not least, and one of my personal favorites is the padlock on a bandana. Folding
a bandana length ways and threading through the lock mechanism, then placing the lock
part in the back pocket provides a battle ready weapon that is quick to deploy and devas-
tatingly effective. Can be carried in separate pieces on a plane, used with a chain as
part of a bike locking rig, and provides excellent reach advantage and deals out gruesome
damage when utilized with speed and power.

Always be ready for a bad situation, and remember: If you're not prepared to do violence,
you're prepared to have violence done to you!

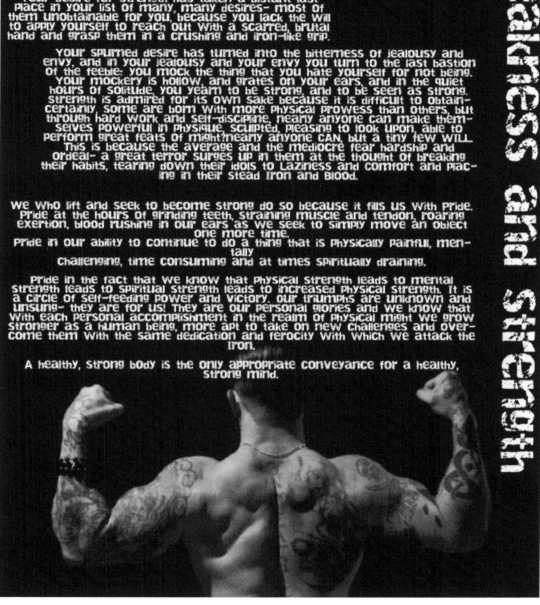

You are weak. Whether you have made a conscious decision to be weak, or because you are
lazy, or because you are afraid of hardship- you are
weak. You do not like being weak. You do not like
being weak because no man likes being weak- it is
part of our evolutionary nature to become strong,
to desire strength, to admire strength, to obtain
strength through mastery over the flesh.
Your desire for strength has taken a distant last
place in your list of many, many desires- most of
them unobtainable for you, because you lack the will
to apply yourself to reach out with a scarred, brutal
hand and grasp them in a crushing and iron-like grip.

Your spurned desire has turned into the bitterness of jealousy and
envy, and in your jealousy and your envy you turn to the last bastion
of the feeble: you mock the thing that you hate yourself for not being.
Your mockery is hollow, and grates on your ears, and in the quiet
hours of solitude, you yearn to be strong, and to be seen as strong.
Strength is admired for its own sake because it is difficult to obtain-
certainly, some are born with more physical prowess than others, but
through hard work and self-discipline, nearly anyone can make themselves powerful in physique, sculpted, pleasing to look upon, able to
perform great feats of might?nearly anyone can, but a tiny few will.
This is because the average and the mediocre fear hardship and
ordeal- a great terror surges up in them at the thought of breaking
their habits, tearing down their idols to laziness and comfort and placing in their stead iron and blood.

We who lift and seek to become strong do so because it fills us with pride.
Pride at the hours of grinding teeth, straining muscle and tendon, roaring
exertion, blood rushing in our ears as we seek to simply move an object
one more time.
Pride in our ability to continue to do a thing that is physically painful, mentally
challenging, time consuming and at times spiritually draining.

Pride in the fact that we know that physical strength leads to mental
strength leads to spiritual strength leads to increased physical strength. It is
a circle of self-feeding power and victory. Our triumphs are unknown and
unsung- they are for us! They are our personal glories and we know that
with each personal accomplishment in the realm of physical might we grow
stronger as a human being, more apt to take on new challenges and overcome them with the same dedication and ferocity with which we attack the
iron.

A healthy, strong body is the only appropriate conveyance for a healthy,
strong mind.

weakness and strength

I awaken from stasis and a life of mediocrity.

I value my health and desire a long and fruitful life.

I will defend myself and my family; my wife...my children, by the strength of my body, my mind and my spirit. I will teach them to do the same.

I am the bodily manifestation of my forefathers, of all my forebears that have preceded me for time immemorial. They lived hard lives in hard eras that have passed into these times of weakness and distraction.

"an iron prayer" by Tim "IZZY" IZYkOWSki

I will live a glorious life and I will earn myself a glorious death.

By the Iron and Blood I am smelted and by the Iron and Blood I am forged anew.

With every breath I draw I seek opportunity for greater strength. With every day I see the deepening results, fruits borne of effort, sweat and experience.

Forever hungry. Forever the glory the 92.

-Jormungandr Division Kommandant

THANKS FOR TAKING THE TIME TO CHECK OUT
IRON AND BLOOD E-ZINE.
IF YOU ARE INTERESTED IN FURTHER
INVOLVEMENT AND INFORMATION.
CHECK OUT THE FOLLOWING LINKS:

operation werewolf blog:
www.operationwerewolfhq.tumblr.com

get outfitted with war-gear:
www.operationwerewolf.bigcartel.com

operation werewolf forum:
www.operationwerewolf.prophpbb.com

:OPERATION WEREWOLF: IS
RABID FUCKING RESISTANCE!!!
XXXXXXXXXX

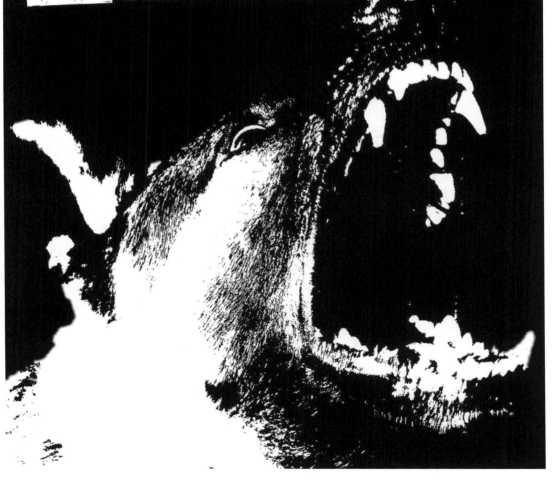

WHAT IS OPERATION WEREWOLF?
OPERATION WEREWOLF IS
RABID FUCKING RESISTANCE!

IRON & BLOOD

XCII

issue no. II

IN THIS ISSUE OF

iron and blood

WE WILL BE EXPLORING SOME
OF WHAT IT MEANS TO RAISE
THE BLACK FLAG OF THIS
ONGOING OPERATION, AND TO
PROVIDE ALL OF OUR READERS
WITH INSPIRATION FOR
THIER DAILY STRUGGLE
AGAINST MEDIOCRITY,
WEAKNESS, BANALITY AND
NORMALCY. THE VERY FACT
THAT YOU ARE READING THIS
TEXT IS A SIGN THAT YOU
HAVE BEGUN SHAKING FREE
OF LEASH AND NOOSE, AND
ARE SEEKING A PATH
THAT LEADS TO
GLORY RATHER THAN
MASS APPROVAL.
FOR WE KNOW THAT THE
ROAD TO LEGEND IS ARDUOUS
AND FILLED WITH MANY A
TRAP AND PITFALL. IT IS
FOR THOSE OF US GROWING
STRONGER TOGETHER TO
OFFER A HAND OF AID TO
OUR STRUGGLING
COMRADES AND
RAISE THEM UP
WITH US...

TO ENSURE THAT THEY, TOO,
ARE ABLE TO STAY THE
COURSE AND FIND THE HERO
WITHIN THEM- IT HAS
SLUMBERED WITHIN US ALL
FOR LONG ENOUGH!

IT IS THIS PRINCIPLE OF
FEROCIOUS MIGHT
AND THE CREATION OF
GODS-AMONG-MEN THAT WE
CALL

operation werewolf

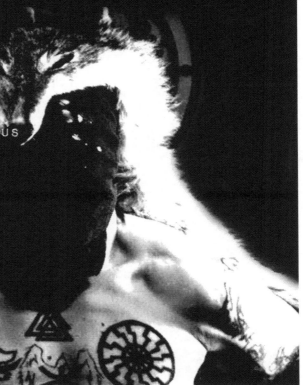

JOIN THE WAR EFFORT!

Iron and Blood 'zine needs YOU!
We are looking for material on D.I.Y. culture,
self-run business, lifting, fighting,
art, and other inspiration for the modern battlefield
OF LIFE.

SEND SUBMISSIONS TO:
WEREWOLFCOMMAND@GMAIL.COM

Anything you think is
valuable to the ongoing
Operation will be consid-
ered for the publication.

If we don't use it, don't get
discouraged— keep sending
in (NEVER SUBMIT), and we'll
do our best to find a spot
for it.

Spread the 'zine to friends,
at the gym, the boxing club,
or wherever you roam in
this burned out waste.

Remember: we're in this
motherfucker together.

THE DUTY OF A HERO

Under a spell of deep slumber, the vast populace of Empire lies DREAMING The dream, however, is cracking at the edges, and through each fracture leaks a profound and un-shakeable DISCONTENT. Discontent, uncertainty, the distinct feeling of enslavement- and anger.

The dream-weavers of Empire create a wondrous woven tapestry of transitory pleasures, the thousand glittering lights of their ILLUSION, each one a different solar system revolving around a great and burning lie: that any man or woman's dreams can be created for them, instead of BY THEM.

Far away from the wretched hovels and muddy streets, the concrete walls, the broken lives and hidden knives that strike in the dark, around marbled tables holding maps crafted from human hide, the Everlasting Council of the Undying Ones convenes. Their ancient rituals of domination and perpetuation have been set since the forgotten dawn of Empire- carefully wrought strategies of control and command, each word they speak spiraling outward to the farthest reaches of their Imperium, these god-kings enthroned on the twin pillars of uncontrollable avarice and never-ending war.

In the small surviving woodlands at the very edges of Empire, other councils are meeting. Savages, barbarians, those tribal leaders who have risen up from the filth and squalor that was their birthright, making of themselves mighty men of renown, reavers and outlaws, warlords whose entire life-stories have been written in blood.

They have not looked to a distant future for the ideal time to congregate and unite themselves under a common banner; nor have they shrugged off the responsibility, leaving it to their children, or their children's children to cast off the shackles of Empire, those chains made of generations of complacency and servitude- chains made of dominion through horror, fear, violence and forced poverty.

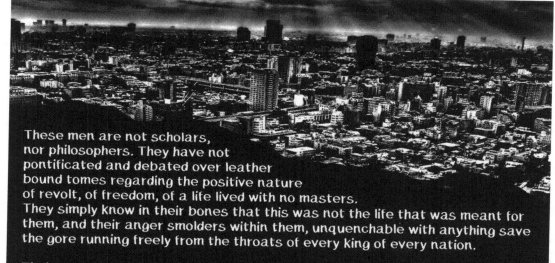

These men are not scholars,
nor philosophers. They have not
pontificated and debated over leather
bound tomes regarding the positive nature
of revolt, of freedom, of a life lived with no masters.
They simply know in their bones that this was not the life that was meant for
them, and their anger smolders within them, unquenchable with anything save
the gore running freely from the throats of every king of every nation.

Their oath has been made to one another. Their tribes have pledged
brotherhood under common cause- to see the rulers and tyrants of this world
gasp out their last while clawing uselessly at spilling entrails, a boot on their
throat, scalp removed from skull and hung from the battle-standards
of a hundred tribes.

The chieftains of these tribes bear a great and terrible weight of responsibility.
They cannot wait for the certainty of victory- for there is no such certainty.
Every year they wait, saying "just a little longer, now," they grow older, the fire
of their spirit burns a little less brightly, limbs grow weaker, hearts less firm in
their resolve, homes more comfortable. They know that a time will not come in
their lifetime that will make this battle easier, so they prepare themselves daily
for the war they will soon wage.

They lift stones the size of foothills, use the very fallen trees of the forest to
make their bodies harder than steel. They run like wild wolves through the
woodlands of their ancestral homes, making war on their rivals with fire, iron,
lead and fist- training their bodies and minds in the ancient ways of brutal
combat, knowing that when the time comes to hurl themselves past the
enemies spear-wall, they will be ready.

They swell the numbers of their tribes with solitary warriors, braves from amongst the ruins on the outskirts of Empire, those who have seen the strength of the **OLD TRIBAL WAYS** and look to become counted among their ranks- these untested men swear oaths of loyalty to their new brethren in **BLOOD AND ASH** out beneath the stars, where trees as old as Empire itself look down in silent approval.

In the dancing firelight, rituals of **EQUINOX** and **SOLSTICE**- these tribes are tied to the land and sky, to blood and old god, sacrificial offerings stain the stone altars black beneath the waning moon and these tribes come together to howl beneath it, calling their far-away kinsmen to **JOIN WITH THEM** in their war against the horror and desolation of Empire.

They cannot hope to win alone, and perhaps, they cannot hope to win at all. But they will prepare themselves for the fight nontheless-

BECAUSE THIS,

SINCE TIME IMMEMORIAL ,

HAS BEEN THE DUTY OF THE HERO.

GO FIGHT!

We're gonna kick this one off with a little Q&A—How many of you have been in a fight? How about in the last 3 years? 6 months?

If you raised your hand to more than one of these, give yourself a pat on the back, especially if you won. This article isn't really directed at you, but you can still probably get something out of it.

I've read a lot about fighting, both on the internet, and in books, because it's a subject that has always fascinated me, from when I was a 14 year old kid afraid of physical confrontation— all the way to a 20 something who couldn't stop fighting, to a 30 something who tries (and usually succeeds) at being more self-controlled.

One of the things that has stuck with me about the very idea of fighting, is that no matter how hard people try, you really just can't intellectualize it. Sure, you can explain what chemicals the brain secretes, or talk about human evolution til you're blue in the face, but until you've beaten someone bloody, or felt your knuckles hit that sweet spot, or your own life taken from you for a few seconds by a devastating shot— you won't get it.

There's a thrill in giving yourself over to violence— from the heart pounding, knee trembling prelude that sometimes comes before a serious threat to life and limb, to the explosive, savage joy of combat, time coming in short clips and images of fists connecting, bodies moving, arms flailing, the sound of bone cracking bone when a hard hit lands. The surge of power that comes from victory, or the shame and crushing weight of defeat.

Too often we get caught up in the idea of fighting, and I think there's a danger in spending too much time fetishizing these things instead of doing them. We run the risk of becoming "armchair experts," those who are able to converse at length about a topic that we have a deep intellectual understanding of, but not necessarily any real-world application.

I've written before lamenting the fact that in our current society, a simple fist-fight can land someone in jail, and how the vast majority of people in general view violence as an abhorrent thing to be avoided at all costs. That's not what I want to focus on here. What I want to talk about instead is what violence and fighting tells us about ourselves, and why it is important to keep it part of our lives- regardless of the risk.

As anyone can probably tell you who has engaged in a brawl while sober, there is a distinct feeling that happens before the first punches are thrown. It is somewhere between fear, anticipation, excitement, joy and panic; a potent mixture of all these, as the adrenaline kicks in and the body prepares itself to flee or fight, tuck tail or knuckle up. What a man does while that feeling has a hold on him will tell you a lot about him as a person.

I said "sober" at the beginning of the last paragraph for a reason- anyone can throw down while the liquid courage is coursing through them, but I've known a hundred loudmouth drunk brawlers who were quiet as kittens when conflict found them without their lucky liquor. Booze removes both clarity and a great deal of our fear impulse, so it doesn't allow you the full measure of a man. Stone cold sober is the way to do it.

The man who can keep his head on his shoulders while the chaos rises is one you want on your side, if possible, and at the very least, its the man we should all strive to be. Because fighting happens less and less in today's society, that experience is being robbed from males, and so when they do find themselves in a violent encounter, they face it with all the fear and uncertainty of deep sea exploration- the first time ain't usually the best time, just ask a girl.

This is reason number one why we need to keep the dust-up a recurring element of our experience...too long removed from the mad embrace of conflict makes us strangers to it. It becomes an "unknown" again, and we are more likely to shy away from it, or to perform poorly, out of reaction rather than action.

We all like to think of ourselves as capable individuals who can brave the worst life has to offer, but many know that deep down, they would run. If we do not place ourselves into the scenario from time to time, how can we know? I am not saying to go out and look for fights, but I am saying to not avoid them if they come your way. By acting a certain way, we strengthen that pathway, and are more likely to act that way in the future. I base my entire philosophy on that one basic idea. So, if we are confronted by someone hostile, and we avoid the situation, citing some excuse we know is total bullshit, like "taking the high road," or "being the bigger man," we will act this way over and over again.

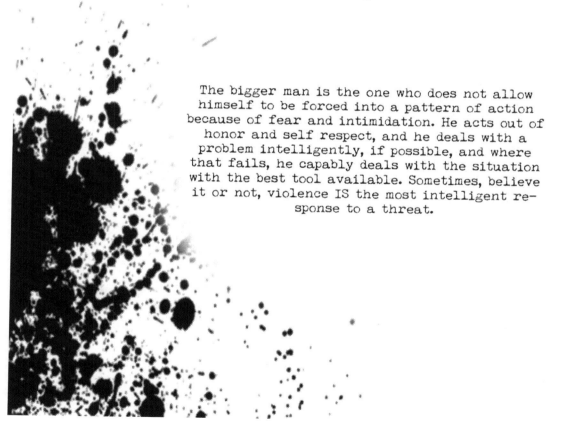

The bigger man is the one who does not allow himself to be forced into a pattern of action because of fear and intimidation. He acts out of honor and self respect, and he deals with a problem intelligently, if possible, and where that fails, he capably deals with the situation with the best tool available. Sometimes, believe it or not, violence IS the most intelligent response to a threat.

I've heard it said that a violent response
only happens when creative communication
fails, and I'd say there's truth to that.
But I'd add to it that sometimes the guy
who is still trying to "creatively
communicate" while getting his fucking
teeth knocked in misread the situation
and deserves what he got.

It's easy for cowards to say that
violence and fighting is the refuge
of the ignorant, or that we as a
species should evolve past it. But
here's a spoiler alert: We won't. We
can't. And you can disagree all day
long, but it won't save you when
someone decides they want what
you've got and are willing to go all
the way.

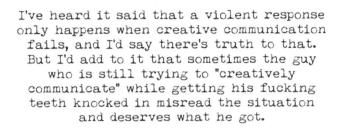

IF YOU AIN'T
PREPARED TO BE
VIOLENT,
YOU'RE PREPARED
TO RECEIVE VIOLENCE.

IF I MUST LEAD OLD FRIENDS
TO BATTLE,
I SING UNDER THE SHIELDS,
AND THEY GO VICTORIOUSLY:
SAFE TO THE BATTLE,
SAFE FROM THE BATTLE,
SAFE WHEREVER THEY ARE...

:salusalu:

Food For Thought

by Edward and Kelsey C.

Too many of us eat like shit.

There's no getting around it: the food we eat is mostly garbage. We all know about the negatives of over-processing, dangerous food additives, and the like. And that's okay in small doses. The human body is an amazing machine capable of enduring some pretty profound wear and tear. But sooner or later, eating like shit is going to catch up to you. You're going to feel run down, your training is going to suffer, and you're going to be packing on weight that sticks to you like glue and refuses to come off. Do it long enough and you'll have things like cancer, diabetic issues, and heart problems to contend with. It behooves you to nip those problems in the bud. But with things like cost and taste being prohibitive factors in eating better, as well as the prevalence of fad diets and scams, it can seem difficult at times to eat well. Fortunately, there are a few tips you can use to eat better, save money, and avoid succumbing to the pitfalls of food selection.

Organic produce is a scam.

With very few exceptions, organic produce isn't better for you. It's still covered in pesticides and a lot of it is imported from sketchy areas where heavy metal contamination is a frequent occurrence. In blind taste tests, organic produce consistently loses to conventional produce more times than not. And for you tree-hugging types, organic farms require more land area to yield the same volume as conventional produce, meaning the shit you eat is actually doing more harm to the environment. Don't fall for the difference in price; it has nothing to do with quality. It has everything to do with popular demand and volume loss due to inferior, outdated agricultural techniques.

If you want to eat better produce, grow your own.

Food from a garden is by every measure superior to food from the store. It's fresher, barely costs anything to grow, doesn't have pesticides, and you can eat it all yourself or barter off surplus for other things you need. Plus, you get a sense of satisfaction from having cultivated your own sustenance. This can be difficult if you don't have land. But there are a number of small kits you can purchase or make yourself that allow for small-scale farming operations even in urban areas.

When it comes to meat, local is better.

Whenever possible, you should avoid eating animals that have been
given commercial feed, hormones, and antibiotics, as well as meat
that's had to travel a considerable distance. The reasons for this are
varied and numerous, suffice it to say that factory farming practices
are a major contributor to eating poorly. For optimal nutrition (as
well as safety), you should stick to meat that hasn't gone through a
great deal of tampering or travel. This can be accomplished fairly
easily if you're lucky enough to live in an area with small farms.
Make friends with the farmers who own livestock: a single animal can
give you enough food to last weeks, even months depending on how
much you're cooking. Failing that, hunting game is a great way to get
high-quality meat that hasn't gone through shipping and processing
before it reaches your plate. Just be careful; some game needs to be
tested for diseases before you eat it.

If you don't live near sources of local meat, you'll have to do some
research. Try to steer clear of chicken that's been injected with
saline or given a vegetarian diet (chickens aren't naturally vegetarian animals). Be wary of beef that says grass-fed but not grass finished, as that means grain has been fed to the animal at some point
in its life. Don't just look at the "organic" label and assume the
meat's high-quality.

Don't neglect "strange" meats.

Bones and organs were a staple of early man for thousands of years.
In today's world, we usually discard them. But these "throwaway"
parts are not only delicious when prepared properly, but they're dirt
cheap and dense with nutrients. Heart is not only delicious, but has
some of the highest concentrations of CoQ10 enzyme in any food available. Cooking with bones can provide essential and often neglected
nutrients like collagen, glycine, proline, and hyaluronan. Even
tongue is packed with B vitamins.

Don't avoid fats.

Many nutrients such as vitamins A, D, E, and K are fat soluble as opposed to water soluble — which means if you're not giving them the proper means to break down, they're not doing shit for you in your body. It's easy to become deficient in all of these if your dietary fat is too low, so be sure to cook foods that are rich in these nutrients with butter or olive oil.

Let it stew.

Cooking is a skill you eventually get good at the more you do it. But as early man figured out centuries ago, sometimes it's less effort and guess work to just chuck everything into a pot. Stews and soups are a great way to combine all your essential foods into one big homogenous mix without having to worry about preparing them wrong. Making stew is particularly useful during colder months when chilly weather can leave you feeling lethargic and unmotivated to put a lot of effort into meal time. It can also be frozen or canned and reheated later, saving you money.

Don't ignore evolution.

Human beings are omnivorous. We're specifically adapted to deriving nutrition from both plant and animal sources. Archaeologists have been able to trace a massive spike in brain development around the same time that we started hunting large ruminant animals, when the abundance of fat and certain amino acid profiles allowed for the enhanced growth of brain matter. In effect: we owe our humanity to the consumption of meat. And while we may not need to eat meat in massive quantities, we're still nutritionally deficient without it.

Many nutritionists and vegans will tell you that it's totally possible to get complete nutrition without animal products, and they're technically right. With proper planning, it is possible. But not only is proper planning rarely carried out, but having a vegan diet with complete nutrition requires heavy reliance upon foods grown with agriculture. Even food grown in a home garden will be insufficient for achieving complete nutrition, so sooner or later a vegan will be forced to complete his diet with food grown on farms. This in turn harms small animals and wildlife, effectively defeating the entire purpose of being vegan.
Replace at least one crappy meal a day with something good.
Sometimes, life gets in the way. It's tough to eat right when you've got a job that demands a lot of your time. But even so, you should make an effort to replace as many shitty meals as you can with good, healthy food. Even changing one healthy meal a day will have a positive effect on your health.

There is no such thing as "human rights." Every day, everywhere, people are bleating like wounded lambs about this "right" or that "right" being infringed upon by some new horror, some tyrannical or fascist oppressor that seeks to take away their precious little whatever-it-is. They have been convinced by the seductive voice of equality and universalism that they are "entitled" to these "rights," such things as freedom, recognition, fairness, leisure and so on. They have been taught that these are realities that no one and nothing should be allowed to take away from them- and it is this exact sense of entitlement that has made modern civilized man feeble, dependent, stomach-churningly weak and incapable.

might over rights

Man is an animal- brutal, savage, violent, aggressive and primal. This is the natural state he has existed in for millions of years, by necessity- but within the State, he is docile, deferential, gentle, passive and servile. He has become so because he truly believes that his "rights" will be defended for him by the benevolent masters who rule his world, those kind and philanthropic members of the Ascended Caste who keep his best interests in mind and pick him up and dust him off when he falls with a warm smile and a helpful word.

He has come to believe that this is natural, and he gnashes his teeth and weeps at the rampant "injustice" still left in the world when some event arises and goes against his carefully planned weltanschauung. He is comfortable in the thought that this will never happen to him, however, and he goes about his life in blissful ignorance of the complete fallacy of his understanding of the world around him, totally unprepared for the eventuality that he will one day come face to face with natural law.

Does the wolf have a "right" to eat a deer, or to live free from the hunter's rifle or the trapper's snare? Does he have the right to be treated equal to the alpha-male? Of course not. He must kill the deer, he must prove to be more than the deer's equal in order to eat and survive. He must evade the bullet, and out-wit the snare. Who will he petition or complain to when he is "unfairly" treated by the other members of the pack? He will not. He will continue to attempt to prove his place through cunning, savagery, ferocity- he will show himself a worthy member of the pack through merit, because in nature, the weak and unfit die, or are cast out.

Why do we as humans feel that we can demand equal treatment with mewling words? We must obtain respect with our actions, not as a right, but with a cold fury, fully capable and willing to display why and how we will demand the treatment we desire- we have to be prepared to fight for our place in this world, to kill for it, if necessary- with the full knowledge that there are those who would kill us without a second thought to our belief in liberty, equality or "fair treatment."

Freedom of speech? Certainly. Say what you like, and decide whether the bullet ripping through your skull was worth it. Recognize that even the spoken word is not a right to speak with impunity, it is a choice you have made and a potential repercussion you must deal with. We have to take responsibility for our actions and understand that in this world, only might makes right.

"ANY MAN WHO TRIES TO BE GOOD ALL THE TIME IS BOUND TO COME TO RUIN AMONG THE GREAT NUMBER WHO ARE NOT GOOD. HENCE A PRINCE WHO WANTS TO KEEP HIS AUTHORITY MUST LEARN HOW NOT TO BE GOOD, AND USE THAT KNOWLEDGE, OR REFRAIN FROM USING IT, AS NECESSITY REQUIRES."
NICCOLÒ MACHIAVELLI, THE PRINCE

"IN DEFIANCE OF DOMESTICATION"
an article by terrence mitchell
(mitchellstrength.co.za)

I desire to see a legion of men stand up in defiance against all that which modernity has foisted upon them in the name of efficiency and functionality and instead embrace all that is considered primal, archaic and visceral - by disregarding all that leads to their downfall - their present-day domestication.

All that is volatile, unpredictable and chaotic - the so-called 'stressors' that were essential for the transmutation of life on this earthly realm and the further evolution thereof.

There is freedom in expression and war is but another form of expression. The alternative is the relative peace and predictability of prison.

Stagnation occurs in confinement - what is confined hence contained can no longer grow, evolve and adapt.

Prison need not be the literal form of incarceration that the majority of people associate with.

Whatever inhibits your personal growth and evolution regardless of its benign and peaceful surface is all too often malignant in nature and rotten to the core; hidden from sight by a cheap veneer of 'stability' that masquerades as 'progress'.

The prison of modernity that has subsequently stripped men of their primal instincts leaving them as mere shadows of their former selves; shadows entrapped in a perpetual vortex of drama, denial and consumerism- an insipid existence where grey is the only colour and none the only number.

I want war- I want total war - I want to rage against an enemy that sees me as nothing more than a potential buyer - a candidate for market research - another good little boy whom by promising to obey the rules and regulations and accept all the terms and conditions is thus integrated into the system.

The same system that is always one more law away from freedom, one more human-right away from equality and one more pharmaceutical drug away from health.

All around me there is endless noise - the mindless chit-chat of talking-heads that spew from their mouths nothing but re-cycled trash verbatim.

I desire to discuss art, literature and phi-losophy - put forth my own questions and in turn share my own answers. Instead I'm subjected to irrelevant statements pertain-ing to mundane events that history shall soon forget.

I desire to make quiet my mind by elimi-nating all sources of white-noise that threaten to distract and entertain me as I make savage my body by the forging of iron with flesh - resulting in a heaving mass of bone, muscle and sinew - able to withstand and prevail over what ever forces of resistance are thrust upon it.

As my contemporaries slide their way into middle-age and take time out of their 'busy' schedules in order to partake in 'grown-up' activities such as house-warming parties, ba-by-showers, couples retreats and Saturday morning trips to the hardware store to pick out paving stones and matching pot plants - I on the other hand - fuelled by an unre-mitting surge of testosterone - am further driven to rebel against all such forms of white-picket fence conformity.

I shall choose experiences over material goods - physical scars over designer labels - worthy and able opponents over meaning-less mass-participation events.

I desire for my life to be a relentless battle as opposed to a weekend fun-run.

I am more aggressive - more passionate - more hungry for knowledge, competition and self-expression than I have ever been in my younger years.

Maybe it's because I've gained some wisdom or maybe it's because I now truly accept and acknowledge that my life is a one-time, never to be repeated deal and therefore with each and every new day I'm indeed moving closer to death and decay - so best I put up a fight!

IN NATURE I TRUST

As more and more people are seemingly content to live longer but albeit more unhealthy lives thanks to a reliance on conventional medicines that promise to cure but never prevent - most probably because cures are always highly profitable while preventions remain essentially free - I choose to live by the rules of nature that although at times appear harsh and somewhat cruel cannot be manipulated nor negotiated with.

Remember that nature much like reality cares nothing for the opinions of mortals and the narratives of institutions.

I choose to live in accordance with the laws of nature even if that means I too shall die in accordance with those same laws.

I shall forgo all the false-foods that are laden with empty calories but devoid of real nutrition much like the many false-prophets of the world whom promise much sustenance yet fail to deliver naught but vacuous truths.

I want to hunt and kill my own food - I want to know that it to had a beating heart and a precious life.

I want to grow my own foods from the soil of earth and watch as the plants thrive in their natural environment.

So perfect in the their imperfections; unlike the equivalents sold in grocery stores - heavily sprayed with a cocktail of chemicals that not only contribute to their flawless appearance but so to their sterile taste.

I desire to travel to distant and wild lands; lands where famous generals commanded their armies; lands where mythical creatures such as giants and dragons supposedly inhabited; lands that were not only carved by the hands of time and the forces of nature but by the hands of the men whom conquered and ruled over them.

OF WOMEN, SEX AND MASCULINITY

As a red-blooded man I too have canal desires. I too wish
to bury my manhood between the lusciously smooth thighs
of a beautiful woman and thrust away with wanton and
reckless abandon.

For this I remain equally unashamed and unapologetic.
However the act of penetrating a women and her subse-
quent submission towards me as the male in that regard no
longer makes me feel any more or less masculine.

I've been for awhile now somewhat indifferent towards the
sexual act in terms of how it relates to ones masculinity.

I am primarily opposed to the often accepted notion of
regarding sexual conquest as a legitimate indicator of
masculine virtue as well as its employment for elevating
or relegating a man above or below his current station
within a hierarchy of men.

Simply put I no longer feel 'manly' when I penetrate a
women.

If sexual conquest was a true indicator of masculine
virtue then we as men willingly place women as the
gate-keepers of our own masculinity.

If for a man to feel like a man - requires access to a
womens vagina - women naturally being the sovereigns of
their own vaginas thus hold the key to now not only
their secret gardens but masculine virtue as well.

I've always considered smooth-talking men - whom with
their slight-of-hand and sharpness of wit were able to
weasel their way into a pair of ladies panties - highly
suspicious.

Furthermore, at least in my experience it has always been
these exact characters whom when the time came to stand-
up and perform manly duties - were the first ones out the
door and down the street.

The saying - every man for himself- was taken literally.

Call me old-fashioned but I choose to judge men on their ability to stand-up and fight
not on their ability to run-away and fuck.
So what makes me feel like a man?

-Reading books and studying the lives of great men from history.
-Training my physical body with other men and sharing my knowledge with these men so
they to can do the same.
-Boxing/grappling/wrestling with other men.
-Competing against other men in various feats of strength and athleticism.
-Making a difference in the lives of other men.
-Taking 100% responsibility for everything within my life.
-Practising 100% self-reliance at all times.
-Spending time in nature preferably in solitude. (most people fear being alone)
-Keeping focused on the work that needs to be done - while the majority of people choose
instead to be distracted and entertained by all that holds them back; preventing them from
achieving what they truly desire.

These are but a few examples. Notice that nowhere does the word 'women' appear.

There are enough pussy-whipped, hen-pecked, domesticated men in this world. Do not throw
your name into the hat and another become.

Sever all ties with the agents of the apocalypse - the engineers of your demise -
the facilitators and overseers of your domestication.

RECLAIM YOUR PLACE AS PRIMAL AND REBELLIOUS MAN IN A ONCE VIOLENT, RUTHLESS AND ARCHAIC LAND.

the TOTENWOLF

THE TOTENWOLF IS THE BANNER UNDER WHICH THE WEREWOLF
LEGIONS MARCH, A DEATH'S HEAD THAT REPRESENTS THE DOOM
OF OUR PERSONAL WEAKNESSES, AND ALL OBSTACLES THAT
STAND IN THE WAY OF THE INDIVIDUAL AND HIS SELF-OVER-
COMING.

ITS SYMBOLISM IS THREE-FOLD: DEATH, THE WOLF, AND THE
SERPENT, WHO WE CALL THE SPAWN OF THE IRONWOOD. WE USE
THESE ANCIENT ARCHETYPES FOR THEIR SYMBOLIC VALUE IN
THE CURRENT AGE, AS WELL AS THEIR IMPACT ON THE INTER-
NAL WORK WE UNDERGO.

IN ORDER TO CREATE OURSELVES ANEW, WE MUST DESTROY
THAT WHICH CAME BEFORE. THE SPAWN OF THE IRONWOOD ARE
REPRESENTATIVE OF THOSE ENERGIES OF DESTRUCTION, THE
ENDING OF CYCLES, THE CLEARING AWAY OF OLD AND CORRUPT
FORMS OF BEING AND EXISTING.

For far too long, practitioners of the Northern traditions have been warned away from working with and experiencing the more ruinous and destructive energies and processes within their own lore- the FEARFUL and FRAIL have pointed an accusatory finger at those few who have explored the darker aspects of this praxis, labelling them outlaws, wolves, anti-nomian creatures of the Other Side;

but the ABLE and INTREPID have always been called so by the servants of rigid doctrine, their explorations and transgressive acts only being made more meaningful by their excommunication from the circle of the "accepted believers."

At the edges of the tamed lands, where the

trembling borders

slowly give way to the howling winds of Chaos- this is the place where we must travel- to look beyond the boundaries and see into that pre-Cosmic void and know its

hidden mysteries.

When we don the **Death-wolf** on our back, or fly its dread banner at our Division gatherings, we are hailing those principles that are the **bloody death** of our old ways of thinking, of doing, of living.

We are hailing our eternal march, **grim** and **war-like**, towards a greater destiny than that which would be chosen for us by those who wear the **crowns of this earth**.

We are signalling to others who are ready for something more, and **calling them** to our **grisly standard**.

Werewolf Legions, unite!

THE CHILL IS ON THE WIND. DARK WINTER HAS ARRIVED. COLD
CREEPS INTO THE LAND AND AIR. AND MANY TURN AWAY FROM
ITS HARSH TOUCH. THEY BECOME SEDENTARY AND SLOW.
UNHAPPY WITH THE NATURAL WORLD. FOR IT HAS MADE THEIR
LIVES MORE DIFFICULT IN SOME WAY OR ANOTHER. THE EARTH
IS DYING: THE YEAR IS ON ITS LAST BREATH BEFORE IT
LIVES AGAIN. AS FAR OFF AS SUCH A THING MAY SEEM.
STILL. SOME FOLK RISE TO THE CHALLENGE OF WINTER.
VENTURING INTO THE FORESTS. MOUNTAINS. DESERTS. PLAINS.
TUNDRA AND CONCRETE CITIES WHERE THEY DWELL.
THESE MEN AND WOMEN CONTINUE THE CYCLE OF EFFORT. LAUGHTER. MUSIC.
STORYTELLING. VIOLENCE. FAITH. LOVE. SEX. FRIENDSHIP. LIFE AND DEATH
THROUGHOUT THE DARK DAYS. THEY STILL STRENGTHEN THEMSELVES. ALLOWING
THE IRON TO MERCILESSLY TELL THEM WHETHER THEY ARE WEAK OR NOT. THEY
STILL TRAIN IN THE CUSTOM OF BULLET. BLADE AND BRAWNY FLESH.
THEY STILL WORK AT THEIR TRADES AND
PRACTICE THEIR CHOSEN CRAFTS AND ARTS-
FOR THE PRIMAL HAPPENINGS OF
THE WORLD ARE HARDLY A REASON NOT TO.

THIS IS BECAUSE WINTER IS NOT A FOE: IT IS PART
OF THE CYCLE OF MANKIND ITSELF. RESPECT IT. BUT
DO NOT PULL AWAY OR CURSE IT. IT HAS MADE YOUR
ANCESTORS. AND IF YOU WISH IT TO MAKE YOUR DE-
SCENDANTS. IT MUST FIRST MAKE YOU.

"winter"
submitted by
a solo operative

THE RED AND WHITE MEANS BLOOD ON THE SNOW. THE GREY SMOKE COMES
FROM THE OPEN BONFIRE OF THE TRIBE RATHER THAN THE DECORATED
FIREPLACE. THE OLD MAN THAT PROWLS THE NIGHT IS THE CRUEL ONE.
CLUTCHING A BLACK SPEAR RATHER THAN A BAG OF GIFTS- THE
BROTHERHOOD OF MEN CHANTING INTO THE AIR AT FREEZING DUSK RATHER
THAN STRANGERS SINGING CAROLS. THIS SHOULD NOT BRING FEAR OR
DREAD. BUT RATHER RECOGNITION AND MEMORY. TAKE HOLD AND MAKE IT
YOUR OWN. OR RATHER RECLAIM IT. BECOME STRONG.

WERWOLF LEGION

WORLD WIDE

THANKS FOR CHECKING OUT THE LATEST ISSUE OF "IRON AND BLOOD."

FOR MORE INFO, APPAREL, INSPIRATION, PERSONAL COACHING AND BLOG: WWW.OPERATIONWEREWOLF.COM

UNITE WITH THE WEREWOLF LEGIONS AT OUR FORUM: WWW.OPERATIONWEREWOLF.PROPHPBB.COM

in this issue:

In the first two issues of this 'zine, the focus was
primarily on the physical aspect of the Operation.
Now, we want to take a look beyond the mundane, at
some of the deeper principles behind what it is we
have set out to accomplish. This may be of interest to
some— for those who are not, NEVER FEAR. Included
here, and coming in the next issue are more strategies
for Division creation, daily regimens for strength,
increasing ones familiarity with violence,
becoming more self-sufficient and so on.

For those intrepid ones, who delve into the fabric of
existence, and seek the deep places and that which is
hidden from plain sight, we hope that the pieces
provided here contain some fuel for your :f:ire.

:3::ALU::9:

IX   II

JOIN THE WAR EFFORT!

Iron and Blood 'zine needs YOU!
We are looking for material on D.I.Y. culture,
self-run business, lifting, fighting, esoterrorism,
art, and other inspiration for the modern battlefield
OF LIFE.

SEND SUBMISSIONS TO:
WEREWOLFCOMMAND@GMAIL.COM

Spread the 'zine to friends, at the gym, the boxing club,
or wherever you roam in this burned out waste.

RUNES part 1.
— Paul Waggener

There are many pieces of writing on the topic of runes, mostly incredibly unsatisfactory in their approach, due in part to a desire to "simplify" the subject matter down to its lowest common denominator. Much of what has been written treats the runes as a simple divination system, like the tarot, and codifies their meanings in such a fashion, even going so far as to have ludicrous ideas like "reverse meanings" and so on. Others have been dry attempts to relegate the runes to a linguistic topic only, claiming that there never was a "magical" use for them, which is, to anyone who has done any study, just as ludicrous.

Many books have been much informed by Kabbalah and other systems of "eastern" magic, which becomes problematic in its own right, but for those authors unavoidable for reasons that will be clear in a few more paragraphs.

First, I will state that in this matter, as in most other things, I am a heretic. My approach to the runes was informed in the beginning by historical work and the writings of others, but has become completely personal through what I would consider to be an appropriate "internalizing" of the runes themselves. Although I can recite the rune poems, and have studied enough Old Norse to attempt my own translations and so on, there was a sort of break from all this at a point of personal revelation.

I threw away all my books on the subject and went through an "unlearning/relearning" process that is ongoing today. We are always beginners with the mysteries contained in the rune rows, and if we are not continually challenging ourselves and our conceptions of them, we has fallen prey to the greatest pitfall on the Road Without End.

This is not to say that those books were useless, in fact, far from it. They served me as a jumping off point from which my own expressions and approach were originally formed. There is simply a time and a place for all things, and at some point, there is a time to go inward.

What we can say, historically speaking, is that somewhere around 2000 years ago, a Germanic individual carved a codified system of characters called runes. They were not simply a linguistic cipher, but a system designed for understanding and codifying the very fabric of the universe.

In the mythology of the Germanic people, this individual was the god Odin, "the High One," whose name literally translates as "the ecstasy/the frenzied one." He did not "invent" the runes, he realized their existence while undergoing a sort of shamanic ordeal which involved "hanging from the World Tree" for nine nights. During this process, he had a revelation, and discovered the runes as the small fragments that act as keys to knowledge of the cosmos itself, massive ideas broken down into manageable pieces.

The exact knowledge imparted by each rune, and by the runes as whole, in combination, and the hidden runes that make up the Count and Tally of a formula, cannot be imparted or understood by a simple explanation. It takes ultimate dedication, meditation, concentration, ritualization, as well as a great deal of time in order to begin opening the locks.

Any information that another human can provide is by its nature, subjective and incomplete, in that it can only resonate within you to a certain degree. Your approach to the runes must be personal, and totally holistic. The runes cannot be understood at first when removed from the cosmology, cosmogony and mythology surrounding them, therefore, a thorough and deep grasp of the Germanic mindset and worldview is a pre-requisite to the serious study and application of these mysteries. This process will and should be ongoing, as new understandings lead to more depth— each time a rune is grasped further, it only deepens. In the words of the one who discovered them, "Each word led me to another word, each deed to another deed."

The study of the runes is an immense undertaking, and immensely rewarding. Those who look to "dabble" in something are advised to look elsewhere. Here, there is no easy hunt, no easy kill. No intuition or greater understanding will be gained.

The word "rune" comes, possibly, from a proto Indo-European source:

Reu— "to roar," and "to whisper," a dual-natured secret is hidden here in plain sight for those who consider its application in the realm of "rune galdr" the vocal process associated with the subject matter. The word rune is found first in use by the Goths in the 4th century, as "runa" meaning "mystery" or "secret." From there it is found in many other languages with a similar or the same meaning.

We will not go deeply into the historical origins or linguistic backgrounds here, as that is beyond the breadth and scope of the current work, and others have done so admirably in the past.

What we do know, is that the runes were used in a ritual, magical fashion, and this is inferred more deeply by the verses found in the Havamal (the Words of the High One, a poem attributed to Odin himself and found in the Poetic Edda.) discussing the eight disciplines of rune-work.

KNOW YOU HOW TO CUT?
KNOW YOU HOW TO CONSULT/ARRANGE?
KNOW YOU HOW TO OBTAIN/RECEIVE?
KNOW YOU HOW TO TEST?
KNOW YOU HOW TO ASK?
KNOW YOU HOW TO SACRIFICE?
KNOW YOU HOW TO SEND?
KNOW YOU HOW TO SPEND?

The so called "Elder Futhark" is composed of 3 groupings of 8 runes each, 24 in all, beginning with Fehu and ending with Dagaz. (There is some argument over this, some end the row with Othala, but it is the opinion of this author that such an arrangement is based on an incorrect understanding not only of the historical facts, but the deeper meanings as well. There are some other arguments involving the placement of the Eihwaz rune as well, this author places it 13th, and does so for reasons described later.)

The "Younger" Futhark came about hundreds of years later, and during that time, intil around 800 CE, the Elder row remained mostly unchanged. The Younger system combines certain runes and their principles together to form a total of 16 runes. The study of which runes were combined and why makes for a very challenging and interesting one.

What will not be done in this series of writings is a systematic, ordered look at each rune, describing its linguistic origins, its basic meanings, as that has been done exhaustively elsewhere. (However, I would recommend that you familiarize yourself completely with not just the better known Old English rune poem, but with the Old Norwegian, Old Icelandic and Old Swedish, as well. The rune poems and their connection to the mythology and worldview is crucial to forming a basis for your own relationships at the beginning of study, and can be essentially used by themselves to inform your work.)

Another reason for not doing things in this fashion is to avoid coloring your own understanding and impression of what each rune "means" by providing you with cookie cutter examples that have been repeated ad nauseum, and instead encouraging you to do your own work.

THE BEST WAY TO KNOW A RUNE IS TO USE IT.

Think about it.

Meditate on it. Examine the word and the shape and the sound, and how it relates to your own life and experience. Go deeper. Consider its place in the mythology, then consider its place in YOUR mythology.

How does this rune combine with another? How do ideas blend and transform, and in so doing, transform you? What we will look to do here is to provide some "jumping off" points, larger ideas that one can consider or discard. There certainly is a system to the runes, and we will go into some of the number correlations and so forth, even those ideas will be merely presented as the result of this author's experience- take it, twist it, burn it, re-shape it. The runes belong to you, but only if you make them yours through KNOWING them. There are many ways to know a thing, and you must use every method available to you to plumb the depths of these great reliquaries of wisdom and awe.

WHAT FOLLOWS IS A BASIC EXPLANATION OF RUNE GALDR

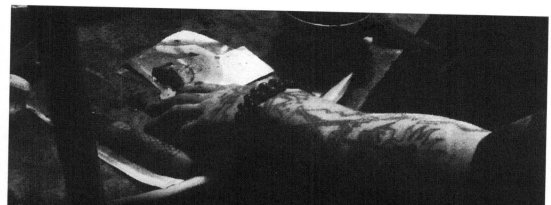

The word galdr comes from a root word meaning "to sing or to chant," but is in the ON (Old Norse) almost always used in context referring to a charm or spell, and became synonymous later on with anything related to the esoteric - the vocal idea of which translates over beautifully to rune-work, as the etymology of this word "rune" can be traced to the PIE (Proto Indo-European) word "reu", which means "to whisper" and "to roar."

Ultimately, the word is first found in 4th century Gothic as "runa", meaning "mystery" or "secret". This vibratory and vocal idea permeates the fabric of Norse myth, beginning with the creation itself. As sparks from Muspellheim and ice from Niflheim come together in the great charged space of Ginnungagap, a form takes shape, which is called Ymir.

The word Ymir comes from an ON root literally meaning "roarer, or roaring one." and from this great, primal representation of matter and force and vitality and wild potential, the realms are shaped by Odin, and his two brothers Vili and Ve, in an act of sacrificial patricide. Just like knowing the root meaning of Ymir, it is helpful to know that the three brothers who utilize this primal force to create, Odin, Vili and Ve, would translate approximately into our language as "Ecstasy, Will and Holiness."

These four combined principles form the groundwork for the thought process and reasoning behind the art of galdr. From this ancient birth of the realm we exist in, we see matter being willfully formed and shaped from a roaring energy, a vibratory and vocal quality that continues to appear later in the mythology.

The main point to note here is that the roaring by itself forms matter, and transforms the environs around it in a seemingly random, haphazard sort of way, but it is only through ecstatic, inspired energy, will, and sacrality, or wholeness, that a conscious forming and directed creative process is able to take place.

This idea carries over to runework directly.in that the rune-forms and sounds by themselves are merely representations- references if you will, to act as a jumping off point for us, a seed from which we can learn, transform, grow, and yes, use to alter, shape and influence our realities, both subjective and objective.

The correlation between vocalization and the runes continues when we look later on in the myths to the point where Odin is hanging from Laerads branches, wounded by spear, and offered to himself in a ritualized sacrifice involving sensory deprivation, pain and fatigue- he peers down into the great depths after hanging there for nine nights, and takes up the runes, the mysteries, the understanding of the universe - and the next verse reiterates this with the famous words "oepandi nam", or " screaming i took them".

With a great roar, Odin takes up the mysteries of the worlds, and with that great vocalization, his understanding dawns, and he falls back from there.
While we attempt to experience this same level of enlightenment, we use the vocal forms of the runes as another way of focusing our energies on them, experiencing them fully by immersing ourselves in the stave forms, the lore, our personal interpretations and understanding of them, the vibratory qualities of their sound, and the effect that all this has on us, the world around us, and the worlds within us.

We use it to bring our will to bear, choosing specific runes to embody certain principles and thought-forms, and bringing those into the objective world by giving them life through sound and sense,- bringing them from the realm of all-potential into the realm of actual being. Each time we perform this act, we are recreating the holy process of the three brothers, using the roaring, Ymir, to shape and alter their surroundings, their perceptions and their understanding of reality in the way they chose.

While our alotted time here does not allow
for us to go completely indepth
into the more advanced workings of
rune-galdr, seid galdr and runic
formula, we can see that the most utilized
form of rune-work is a vocal one- although
bindrunes and the like can be carved and
stained, and carry a great
power on their own, it is primarily through
the use of galdr that these staves
are understood and actualized on a mystical
level- the same can be seen when
loading mead, or singing pre-written formulae
during the course of ritual and
so forth.

There are many runic formuale that have
been discovered on various
stones, bracteates, amulets and the like, and
each of them can be studied and
utilized in rune-galdr, as well as formulas
of one's own design- in order to
fully understand and craft one's own runic
formula for use in galdr, there are
some basic principles to keep in mind:

Throughout the runic aetts, we see that
in each aett, there are two vowel forms, each of which represents a core
element or property, that can be combined with the more wide and expansive
consonant seeds to form complex and layered formula, or working words, which
act sort of like the mantras seen in present zen and yogic techniques.

Through continued practice and application, there are essentially limitless
combinations and principles that can be used to empower and deepen our practice.
When creating these formulae, we can look to some historical ones for a better
understanding of how this can be done most effectively.

As an example of how this functions we will look at the :luwatuwa: formula,
originally found on the Vadstena bracteate discovered in 1744.
The translation of this word is generally taken to be "to the earth, to the sky,"
but deeper meanings can be plumbed when we look at its qualities in vocal galdr.
When sung in a repetitive manner, new words form themselves in and around the
root-word, a deliberate tool which can be seen in other runic formulas such as
:lathu: as well as other IE sources in general. (For example, scholars of the
Bhagavad Gita have stated that the best way to understand the Gita is to simply
vocalize the word over and over, until natural rhythm turns the word into "Tagi."
which means "one who has renounced everything for God.")

Using this technique within the luwatuwa framework, we can hear a vocal shift in
between repetitions, and the hidden word :ALU: is heard.
So, in this case, we can hear another rune-formula, the popularly inscribed
"ALU", within this greater principle. Beside this we can see that there is
generally a consonant/vowel/consonant/vowel format, or vice versa, rather than
stacking multiple consonants or vowels in a row.

Due to this, we can break down the meaning of a formula even more.
For example, many are familiar with the Gebo Auja bindrune-
combining the two runes :G::A: together for a meaning of "luck or gift from the
gods." On helmets and spears have been found the inscription G A G A G A.
We can probably surmise that the formula is not intended to be taken as the word
Gagaga, but rather as a formulaic representation of the words Gebo Auja,
sort of a runic acronym, if you will.

Galdr is truly a powerful tool, and can offer the practitioner not only a
deeper understanding of the runes themselves, but their relations with one
another, their vibratory force, and their uses and practical application within
the greater work of runic study and esoteric runology in particular. Through
it's use we can weave a mighty song, and finally begin to ask ourselves the
important question: "What would we change, and Why?"

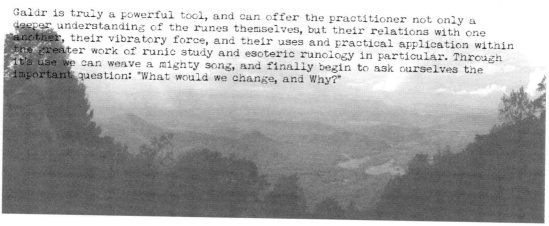

Death Ritual

APPALACHIAN CROOKED PATH CONJURE WORK
TO THE GREATER GLORY OF KING DEATH.

CUSTOM APPAREL, INCENSE BLENDS, JEWELRY, ART,
ALTAR TOOLS AND MORE.

WWW.OPERATIONWEREWOLF.COM/DEATHRITUAL

THE HIDDEN BLADE
-MIKE BLACKGRAVE

THE VAST MAJORITY OF PEOPLE HAVE NO IDEA HOW TO USE A KNIFE IN VIOLENCE. THEY BASE WHAT THEY SHOULD DO ON WHAT THEY SEE VIA TV, MOVIES, AND SADLY, VIDEO GAMES. IN TRUTH, THE USAGE OF A KNIFE IN VIOLENCE IS VERY EASY IF YOU AVOID ONE ELEMENT: DUELING. THE DUEL TAKES A HIGH MODICUM OF SKILL IN MANY FACETS TO BE SUCCESSFUL, BUT IN REALITY IT IS A DANGEROUS WAY TO LOSE YOUR LIFE NO MATTER THE SKILL LEVEL.

THE ABILITY TO USE STEEL IN VIOLENCE COMES DOWN TO WILL AND OPPORTUNITY. WITHOUT WILL, ALL ELSE IS MOOT. IF YOU CANNOT BRING YOURSELF TO WIELD IT WHEN NEEDED, THEN NO AMOUNT OF TRAINING WILL AID YOU ON THE DAY IT ALL GOES BAD. THE OPPORTUNITY TO USE STEEL IS A SELF CREATED WAY, YOU HAVE TO BE ABLE TO DECIDE WHEN IT'S TIME TO GO TO STEEL, AND HOW TO GET TO THE STEEL. THERE ARE MANY FACETS OF CARRY. MANY PEOPLE CARRY FOLDERS, AS IT IS AN EASY WAY TO EDC (EVERY DAY CARRY) A SMALLER KNIFE. THE PROBLEM ARISES WHEN IT IS EASILY VISIBLE DUE TO THE CLIP- IN A PINCH THAT VISIBILITY MAY NULLIFY THE USAGE OF THE STEEL BECAUSE IT IS NOW A FOCUS OF THE ENEMY AS WELL AS YOURSELF. A FOLDER IS NOT ALWAYS THE EASIEST TO GET OUT AND INTO ACTION WHILE IN A FRAY. IF ACCESS- ING AND OPENING THE KNIFE ISN'T PRACTICED, IT CAN BE A NIGHTMARE UNDER DURESS TO GET IT IN THE FIGHT. THIS IS WHERE THE HIDDEN BLADE METHODOLOGY SHINES- THE USAGE OF SMALLER FIXED BLADES PLACED ON THE BODY VIA SHEATHS IN AREAS THAT ARE EASY TO ACCESS UNDER DURESS.

The Tools
Short bladed knives, kerambits, spikes. I personally keep the blade length to four inches or under. I also prefer kydex sheaths over leather for the simple reason that they last, and stay firm. I use 550 cord lanyards if the blade will be deployed around the neck, or as a "pop n go" rig.

Where
My personal preference for hidden blade is on the waistline, tucked deep in the waist. This is where a kydex pop n go rig using 550 paracord comes into play. Another hideaway place that works well is the famous neck knife- paracord works well for a lanyard. This method takes solid work to get fast and good at deployment. Lastly there is the "up the arm" hide. This method uses clear packing tape and a very short blade- I use the Irish Sgian Dubh dirk for this method. The method is fantastic to use when you are expecting trouble. It is an easy hide and lightning fast to deploy. I am not a big fan of boot knives- to me it is a very slow process to obtain the steel and get it into a fight. There is a lot that can go wrong drawing from so low.

When
When should you use the blade? That question is only answerable by the individual in the battle. One must remember that we live in a society of laws- laws that will hem you up for life if you are not careful. My advice to anyone is to know those laws, and make sure that when you use steel you are as close to "right" as you can be- and even then it may not be enough. Know the law, lawyer up always, and keep your mouth shut. Do not allow yourself to be a statistic. In violence there is one story: your story, end of story!

How

THERE ARE MANY SCHOOLS OF THOUGHT ON KNIFE USAGE. SOME SCHOOLS TEACH
THE DUEL AND LITTLE ELSE, OTHER SCHOOLS TEACH EVERYTHING FROM A READY
POSITION, WHERE FLASH RULES THE DAY AND PRACTICALITY TAKES A BACK
SEAT. I HIGHLY SUGGEST YOU AVOID THESE SCHOOLS. IN TRUTH THE USAGE OF
THE KNIFE IS SIMPLE. IN SEAMOK I USE CUTTING PATTERNS AND THRUSTING
PATTERNS THAT COINCIDE WITH ONE ANOTHER. THESE PATTERNS ARE DESIGNED
TO TEACH STUDENTS HOW TO USE THE ANGLES, AND HOW TO INTEGRATE THEM
WITH SOLID FOOTWORK AND BODY MECHANICS. IT IS NOT HARD, ONLY DEMAND-
ING. IT DOES NOT TAKE A LIFETIME TO BE GOOD WITH STEEL, YOU CAN BE
GOOD IN A FEW DAYS IF YOU WORK IT. IT ALL COMES DOWN TO WILL.

ONCE THESE PATTERNS ARE INGRAINED, ONE MUST NOW GO INTO THE FRAY AND
FIND OUT HOW THEY WORK FROM VARIOUS SITUATIONS (ALWAYS USE TRAINING
BLADES). THIS IS WHERE A SOLID TEACHER AND TRAINING PARTNERS COME INTO
PLAY. THEY CANNOT GIFT WRAP EVERYTHING FOR YOU- YOU MUST FAIL IN
TRAINING TIME AND TIME AGAIN WHILE SWALLOWING THE EGO AND BUILDING
YOUR SKILLSETS. YOU MUST FIND OUT WHERE TO HIDE YOUR BLADES ON YOUR-
SELF AND DO SO, THEN START SLOWLY AND METHODICALLY DRAWING THEM. HIDE
YOUR TRAINING BLADES IN THE SAME MANNER AND GO ONE ON ONE WITH YOUR
TRIBE AND FIND OUT UNDER DURESS HOW EASY OR HARD IT IS TO GAIN ACCESS
TO THEM. IN TIME YOU MUST ALSO BUILD SCENARIOS OF MULTIPLE OPPONENTS,
USING THE HIDDEN BLADE METHODS ONCE YOU MAY BE GROUNDED, AND ALSO WHEN
YOU ARE AMBUSHING. THE AMBUSH IS FROWNED UPON BY MOST SCHOOLS, I PER-
SONALLY FEEL IT IS THE BEST AND SAFEST WAY TO USE THE KNIFE. A KNIFE
IS AN AMBUSH WEAPON!

You will see by learning the cutting and thrusting templates that the blade fits everywhere. It has a point and a sharp edge—whatever it touches, it will destroy. The key in combat is being able to create that opportunity under duress to access the blade and then let your raw aggression naturally drive it home, whether that be by slash or thrust. Often times the way we intend for it to go down doesn't happen, things happen in violence, but rest assured a vicious slash is just as dangerous as a deep thrust, and if you've done your work you'll know that one follows the other.

Keep it tight, in your zone, use your skills, hone your will, chin down, breathe, train, and do!

It is your life on the line. Know your tools, where to hide them, when to deploy them, and how to use them. This all happens in the Ludus (training hall) and that hall is wherever you put your feet.

"Steel opens minds."

- M.B.B.

92

BEYOND RAGNAROK:
LOOKING BEYOND DESTRUCTION
BY CHASE SUDRLAND

In conversations with young men, the subject of wishing for the apocalypse seems to be a constant. It's amazing, fanciful, dreamy, and illustrious for them. In pop culture, in the underground, in video games, young men everywhere are secretly wishing for the collapse of the civilization so they can shed the tedious and over-regulated lifestyles that they consciously know are not healthy or rewarding for them and turn into a zombie hunting bad-ass that gets all the chicks. A large problem I always see first, and point out to these young men, is that they either have a single skill, a poor commercial adaptation of a single skill, or no skills outside of the service economy at all. They have almost no wealth outside of the monetary system, or techno-babble gadgets (no hand tools, no weapons, no exercise gear, not even clothing for life beyond clubbing and work) and a work ethic that is barely passable, or completely absent..

There is this illusion that the collapse will be just a free ride for all, and that all of the sudden everything is going to be a total chaos with no ramifications for any behavior and that suddenly, we will all instantly become "warriors" and it will be totally awesome- just like in the movies, right?

I hear it all the time:
"Oh man, society isn't worth preserving so I'm just gonna take what I can and live it up, and when it goes to shit, I'll come over then!"

"Yeah man, it's fantastic that you are doing what you are, when shit hits the fan, I am totally comin' down to help out and live with you!" "Oh man, if everything collapses, I'm moving into your neighborhood!"

What those statements actually say is this: "Man, I am a selfish cunt and I am going to try and emotionally blackmail you into accepting me into your community on my terms, as I am enjoying the ride of my life of just taking everything I can without respect or discipline."

"I want you to do all the hard work first so I can come and reap the benefits. That's how it all works in the movies, some guy builds it and then the people come and every-one lives in total utopia right?!" "I don't care that you are now connected to this place by blood and soil, I am a modern person and I should have the freedom to just move into any community that I want and you just have to accept me!" ...and the list goes on.

I am reminded of the story of the grasshopper and the ant. To summarize; In the beginning the grasshopper and the ant were friends. The ant worked hard all summer and prepared for winter and the grasshopper partied his ass off, assuming that his friendship
would be all that he needed to facilitate the ant helping him out when the winter came.
Well, the winter came and the ant refused and the grasshopper froze to death with the
future he chose. This is true in life too. Commitment means 100%. A lifestyle change
cannot be on the surface, it must be a deep and meaningful shift towards a state of being
supported by a cultural inclination and a philosophical standard, or else it's just posing.

Like all of the other propaganda for OPWW, I will repeat the main message: You must
transform yourself entirely to embody the foundation for the energy that you wish to
manifest into the world. You cannot pray your faults away, and you cannot yell out into
the universe your wishes and expect someday that someone will come along and pay to make
your life work for you so that all you have to do every day is just "experience".

Reality will crush you, and the natural world will eat your corpse,
and you will deserve it. What these "hopeful friends" are wishing is for someone
else to do the work for them, because deep down, they actually believe that it's someone
else's job and that their personality will make them valuable for the community; because
that's what they've been programmed to believe all of their comfortable and safe lives.

What these hopeful friends need to hear, is that they have no place in this world and
they aren't welcome without 100% commitment. Their excuses are weak as fuck, and their
convictions non-existent. If you have people in this life inside an exclusive inner
circle space in your community, they should have earned it by digging in the dirt with
you, planting the seeds with you, building the hall with you, building yourselves with
each other. Iron and Blood. Talk is cheap, and actions are accurate pictures of honest
intent. If you let someone into your inner circle without them taking the necessary
action to pass those tests, they will compromise you, and they will bring your community
down in some form because they were not present for the manifestation of its being.

"Better to make not a sacrifice, than too large of one." - Havamal. Sometimes it is better
to make them reach out, than to reach out yourself.

LIVE LIKE THE COLLAPSE HAS ALREADY HAPPENED.

Now I will speak for the initiated: It is hard sometimes shedding the skin of the old life. The comfortable life, the motions of habit and the ease of what was familiar- but in that life we knew that things were wrong, unfulfilling and usually meaningless. Looking back should only be done to measure how far you've come, not to retreat or beat old corpses. With new changes come new challenges.

In my own life I have been able to conquer the need to look back by maintaining my focus on my goals instead of myself. This way I am always thinking about what I am achieving instead of what I am being. It is too much internal focus that often turns a man into a bucket of sour soup. So with this, I say it's time to live as if the collapse already happened. Tools, skills, tribe, personal rebirth, training, strife, growth, challenge, and finally, glory, should be the focus.

Instead of buying beer, save up for a new power tool, a weight bench, a set of boxing gloves. Instead of smoking, buy a packet of wrenches, screwdrivers or other useful tool every week. Make a forge, learn how to manipulate metal, make a belt driven wood lathe and make your own dishes out of logs you cut down in the forest. Along with the comfortable life comes addiction to the internet to waste time and be distracted. The double edge to this is that the internet offers everything a person needs to become absolutely glorious. Go on the classifieds, seek out old hard-asses and learn their skills. If they say no and it's something worth learning just show up until they give you something to do. Hang out. I've learned more this way in my life than ever seeking out "employment." If they abuse you, then leave and find another opportunity. Don't take failure personally, and don't put forward an image greater than what you are. Lift, fight, grow, become. Start the world.

TANK DESTROYER

RECORDS & DISTRO

TDdistro@gmail.com

www.discogs.com/seller/TankDestroyerDistro/profile
www.ebay.com/usr/tankdestroyerdistro
tankdestroyer.bigcartel.com

SUPPORT TANK DESTROYER
RECORDS AND DISTRO!

the Nightbringer CULTUS:

Considerations on Magic and the Occult

A DISTILLATION AND SUMMATION
COMPRISED OF EXCERPTS FROM VARIOUS
PUBLISHED AND UNPUBLISHED INTERVIEWS

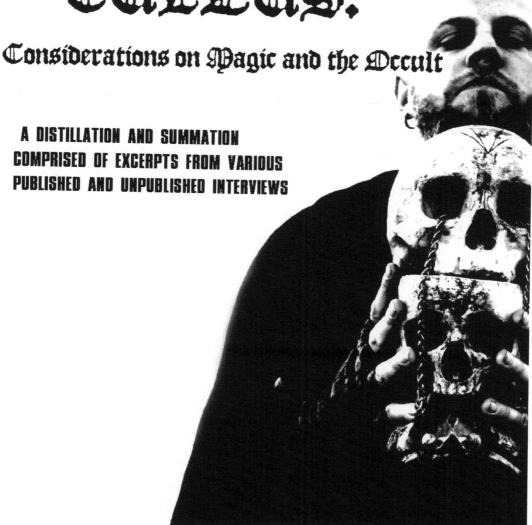

On Death, Nigredo and the Initiatic Path
- Naas Alcameth

"The symbol of the 'path', in the context of initiation, is ineffable as
it expresses movement that is really no movement at all, yet can be
expressed symbolically by way-markers that signify stages of
profound personal transformation. We have expressed these stages in
the form of a trinity that at once represents the path itself as well
as comprising a certain divine name integral to this path. The three
phases can be directly linked to the predominant phases of the Great
Work of alchemy. To briefly surmise, the path denotes a
transformation from a state of purely gross or profane 'existence', the
mundane state in which most live out their lives day by day, into a
state of gradual dispersion of the profane self within utter
darkness, trial and undoing, a necessity requisite to reach a moment
Jung dubbed the enantiodromia (the term not to be limited here by the
boundaries of psychology but to be understood in the truly spiritual
sense), the great epiphany that is said to be both the moment of one's
death (of the profane self) and one's rebirth (into true life). Thus the
path entire is defined by progressive states of becoming towards a
state that could be described as perfected Being, a state that would be
beyond comprehension of the purely human intellect alone. With that
said, let it now be expressly stated that we in no way can lay claim
to any true knowledge of this state of Being (to know is to be!), only
the theoretical knowledge thereof which is ultimately inadequate in
and of itself, so we must be careful how we speak about such things
and only in proper accordance to our current relation towards such
things, that is from our position below to that which still remains so
vastly above (and yet within), from worshiper to worshiped. As I have
stated elsewhere, we may speak of the shadow of the thing but not the
thing itself and to attempt otherwise is to do ourselves and any who
would read or hear our words a great disservice and debase what we
tell you is personally sacred as to do so would be to speak of the
sacred with the tongue of sophistry, intentional or no.

We still yet toil in the black soil of Khem, we suffer in the underworld and bleed in the Dark Night of the Soul and could tell you but a little of the actualized truth of the light beyond the death that must come, the great epiphany we seek in the nadir of the abyss and our own destruction. As if such a thing could be relayed anyhow. However much can now be said here about what is dubbed 'intuition', the true Intellect, that 'voiceless voice' that is too often drowned out by the cacophony of ego, vanity or the ever deafening language of 'modern reason'. This 'intuition', is rectified through those fleeting yet sacred moments of vision and experience afforded to us via meditation, incubation, dream and practice, and thus serves to further affirm the voice that speaks without word. The rest is a matter of faith, a faith that arose and crystalized from our natural spiritual constitution to begin with, and the very prayer of the 'voiceless voice' that is the guiding daimon, the intuition'.

With this kept in mind, the lyrics represent both our real experiences within our initial black work, the actualization of our faith, and the forward projections of our highest aspirations, our longing and desire that will carry us onward into the ineffable night of our 'other-becoming'.

Thus the lyrics should be inter-preted as our promise and decree and the vehicle of our worship and praise of that which is above us, below us and hidden within us.

"...one must "learn to die". This death is no less than the journey into the underworld, the Hermetic nigredo and dissolution of the ego, the initiation within the house of Hell. This concept is fairly universal in ancient religion and can be found in other writings from both the East and the West. Certain Pre-Socratic texts such as Parmenides and Euripides express this concept vividly... What we construe as life, is no life at all, it is largely illusory with only fleeting moments and vestiges of true life, mere fragments of the vastness that is beyond what we know as life. The path to awaken, towards living is the path that leads one to death, a death in life to obtain life in death, to die before you die that you may eternally live, and this life is something that we can't possibly conceive of with our intellect and would bear no semblance to what we know as life.

We are painfully aware that we are still very much asleep, still strug-
gling for an inlet that may lead us to the possibility of reaching the state that could lead one to real awakening. To realize this (which short of the actualized experience itself, we can only do
conceptually, which is no real knowledge at all really) is the greatest burden one can conceive of as the need for "salvation" from this state assails you with the most profound sense of immediacy. The prognosis is terminal and the cure requires a Herculean task, to "learn to die". This all might seem very paradoxical, but truth, it is said, has a tendency to lie at the crossroads where opposites meet..." — Naas Alcameth
-Taken from L'Antre Des Damnés. 2014.

"...I will ... speak to it as humbly as is proper. As stated above, we are all very much dead already. We are as dead as everyone else around us, the only difference being that we are somewhat aware that we are dead, we are aware, as much as one can hope to be while in this state, of our utterly soporific condition. We have admitted it in our heart of hearts, yet this knowledge is no real knowledge at all and is nigh useless without action, and the action required of us is nothing less than "learning to die"... So we have to look inward, pray, meditate, worship, be still and silent, be patient and determined and we must hope to realize and to do so much more than all of that as so much more is demanded and we have hardly taken a single step in the dark let alone set foot in the land of the dead. We are still at the onset of nigredo, struggling in the grip of the world and the strangle hold of ego, to realize even a fraction of what one must know before taking yet another step. We have accepted the burden of this truth and regardless we push forward into the night, into the desert, into the ocean to die. Death thus becomes both our judge and our messiah, our salvation and our damnation." — Naas Alcameth
-Taken from L'Antre Des Damnés. 2014.

On Will and Lawlessness:

"The sidhas and wild Aghoris come to mind here and are perhaps prime examples as they approach the breaking of worldly bonds via the breaking of moral, societal and spiritual norms, by upholding a codex of opposition towards said laws, a mode which is refined and specific towards their spiritual path. However, "lawlessness", when pertaining to one's self and conduct, can vary wildly in interpretation, and will often prove to be the most spiritually fatal of paths for all but the very few, as such an embracing more often than not creates bonds to the lower world instead of destroying them.

If one can approach a path of "lawlessness", such as vamachara, in a manner that is always contemplative and detached, then perhaps they will have a great deal of success. Needlessly seeking out "victims", or needlessly doing anything for that matter denotes lack of will, obsession or attachment. Being without personal codex denotes lack of will and laziness. One can be "lawless" towards the world while striving to maintain a higher inner law, yet even this approach can eventually create enslavement, the enslavement of self to that which is not self, or the "Other".

All of this, when applied to the concept of god (the term used in the Platonic/Orphic sense), leads into the debate between kataphatic and apophatic theosophy, which we have touched upon in previous interviews. I lean towards the later approach. Yet to embrace this fully one must inevitably immolate all sacred laws and self-pantheons in an endless succession of constant creation and destruction in order to be forever liberated. This leads to paradox, yet as stated elsewhere, paradox is the point where true wisdom is revealed. Regarding "victims", upon the path I have chosen, one's self is one's own sacrifice, a sacrifice that requires no "victims" besides the self, which must be killed again and again. To fail to achieve this one then becomes the "food for the gods", the true "victim", so to speak."

— Naas Alcameth
—Taken from an unpublished interview. 2014.

"Various Sufis and their schools have many times ventured on the edge of the publically accepted or understood. For instance, Mansur al-Hallaj usually is referred to in Sufi lore as an example of a gnostic who spoke of such things that are better to remain hidden within the esoteric communities and thus had to face the gallows for his act of heresy. I would not really say Sufism as such (which obviously is or ever was any homogenous tradition either) have had any direct influence on the work of Nightbringer, although we are intrigued by some of the various forms "heretic" or heterodox practices and theological ideas connected to some of the traditional saints. It's quite interesting to see that when genuine spiritual gnosis is made available to the public by true prophets it usually is frowned upon by the established order, thought as "evil" and "destructive" or simply as viewed as madness. We are of the belief that the Divine does not shelter its essence from Darkness or the Abominable, yet actually is best understood through it. This is also the secret that many of the Sufis hinted at when they traveled to the ruins outside of the city, to the forbidden taverns and brothels, befriended the shaitan and djinn, in search for God outside of the common religious order."
-- Ar-Ra'ad al Iblis
-Taken from the interview with heathen Harvest. 2014.

"...what might be thought of as "darkness" to some might actually be "light" to others. Or even more so, that which some actually is common to describe as "dark" might actually be the most brilliant light that but casts the greatest shadow about it. This is not saying that it is "profane", but rather actually ascribing sacred properties to it... The Sufis were said to indulge in wine. But this was not at all the wine of the profane type, but a symbolic wine of ecstatic love. The problem however is that it is symbolized by actual wine, the very profane type that is found in the forbidden tavern in the wastelands outside of the ancient cities. There were in other words something highly alluring about using such allegories, about deconstructing the images of the common religious order and indeed seeking the Divine in what we may call "Darkness" in order to UNDERSTAND it better than in the light of day (read: conventional forms of worship). If I may quote Crowley here:

'Not by the pipings of a bird
  In skies of blue on fields of gold,
But by a fierce and loathly word
  The abomination must be told.
The holy work must twist its spell
From hemp of madness, grown in hell.'

- Ar-Ra'ad al Iblis
-Taken from an unpublished interview. 2014.

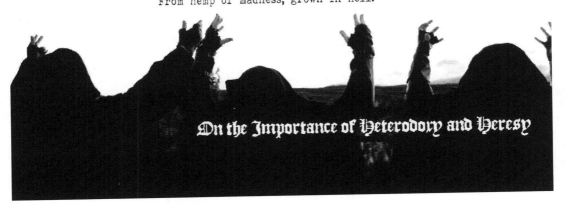

On the Importance of Heterodoxy and Heresy

On the Twilight of the Kali Puga:

"..It should also be noted that the ancient world simply could not per-
petuate as there is a divine cyclic law that governs all, and decline is
simply a part of the natural process. Everything that is not fixed in
eternity, everything that exists within the world of multiplicity, dies.
It dies in order that other things may be reborn. Men, civilizations and
entire ages, all die."
– Naas Alcameth
–Taken from Interview with Metal Hammer (DE). 2014.

"We believe this (the arrival of the Twilight of the Kali Yuga) beyond a
shadow of a doubt and any who cannot plainly see the reality of this are
blinded to the world around them by the world around them, which is
often the case unfortunately. We are in the Twilight of the Age of the
Wolf, and decline in every sense and on every conceivable level is
inexorable. This is the ontological nature of all, death and
birth/rebirth. Things are exactly as they must be. In the age of lead all
one can do is to safe keep the gold within their heart."
–Naas Alcameth
 –Taken from L'Antre Des Damnés. 2014.

WOLVES DEN PRINTING

SCREEN PRINTING
EMBROIDERY

502-417-9537

@WOLVESDENPRINTING
FACEBOOK.COM/WOLVESDENPRINTING
WOLVESDENPRINTING@GMAIL.COM
WWW. WOLVESDENPRINTING .COM

Stadagaldr

A Formula of Physical Runework
By Paul Waggener

Stadagaldr

A Formula of Physical Runework
By Paul Waggener

Photography by Diana Saunders
Assembly & Misc. Editing originally by Danielle Fedorshik
Re-Editing by Francisco Albanese

The following brief work is an attempt to give the beginning practitioner a firm grasp of the staðas, that is, physical positions of the rune staves themselves, as well as a solid starting point for their own explorations in this powerful tradition. It is based on my own work and experiences, and is in no way intended to be an exhaustive look at the topic, nor a historical or anthropological textbook arguing personal points of view.

Those individuals who reject staðagaldr as being a foreign influence on the Northern tradition or Indo-European practice in general need look no further than the Rig Veda, the oldest written work in any I.E. language, or do some cursory studies on the Indus Valley civilization from which the text originated. There can be little doubt that what is today known as "yoga" (from the Sanskrit word meaning "to bind together," or "to yoke") was practiced in many forms throughout the ancient Indo-European world, and beyond. To think that advanced breathing, mental, spiritual and physical exercises are solely the province of the Asian culture is not only insulting, but ignorant and those heathens and vitkar of Indo-European stock would do well to take more time to explore their own history outside of Northern Germany and Scandinavia — although even there, the remnants of the tradition can be found in such artifacts as the Gallehus horn.

The ultimate aim of this work, and what the continued intensive practice of the methods outlined herein can offer the vitki is simple: to unite all areas of the soul complex into a cohesive unit through breathing control, physical positioning, deliberate intention and spiritual exercise, combined with the vibratory and magical effects of vocalized runes, formulae and so on, generally referred to as galdr. Furthermore, the work you hold provides a fresh look at the runic staðas from a more dynamic and flowing position.

In all, it is hoped that with this modest work, new blood can be injected into the veins of what has in recent years become a largely intellectual practice filled with armchair magicians and tired old men who would rather debate and critique than attempt and succeed. Those interested in the techniques herein, and Germanic magical practice in general are advised to seek out the Inner Hall of the Galdragildi with a serious mind, a pure intention and an Inner Fire.

— Paul Waggener
Yule 2010 CE

CHAPTER ONE:
THE SOUL AND THE TREE

THE GERMANIC SOUL COMPLEX

To begin the work of unifying all aspects of the being, those pieces must first be identified. Similar to the way the runes can be used to separate the cosmos (and everything within it) into principles and ideas that relate and correspond to one another in myriad ways, the same can be done with all the facets that make up the mind, body and spirit; in fact, in Northern European thought, there was no division between the three — rather, they were all integral parts that blended together to give life and form to the individual. The Gemanic peoples had their own unique concept of the soul, which looked at as nine parts: Lík, Hamr, Fylgja, Hugr, Minni, Önd, Óðr, Hamingja, and Sál.

A quick overview of these terms reveals the following basic information regarding each. This is not intended to be a full treatise on the subject, merely a brief introduction to soul-lore in the Northern Tradition:

Lík refers to the physical body, the literal flesh and blood. As such, it is no less holy or integral a part of the being than any other, and in fact many Indo-European peoples perceived the body as a vehicle of the holy fire of önd, the temple that houses the sacred flame. It should be treated with all the respect and care that such a comparison implies, and when placed into alignment with all the other soul-parts, can function at its highest ability.

The hamr is the "mode of being," or spiritual persona. In the lore discussing shape-change or "hamhleypa," what is being referred to is a change in hamr, a switching of the spiritual body, not an actual a physical change — although some sagas (such as that of King Hrolf Kraki) do indeed speak of lík-change. The harm is, however the metaphysical body, and as such be altered and changed by one who is "shape-strong," or hamramr. This subject is a deep one, with many approaches and is outside the scope of the present work.

The fylgja or "fetch" is, for lack of better terminology, one's protective or guiding spirit, usually personified by a being of the opposite sex or an animal connected to the individuals psyche in a strong way.

The hugr is the rational, conscious mind. The intellect, or thought process which works in close tandem with the minni: that which remembers.

Önd is the breath of fire, given by Óðinn to Ask and Embla, and is discussed in more detail in the following chapter.

Óðr is the ecstasy represented in the name of its master, Óðinn. It is the divine madness of strife, poetry, music and sexual frenzy — this is a potent energy which the experienced can tap into in order to elevate the consciousness and work potent ritual of many kinds.

Hamingja is one's accumulated personal power. Including that of his family and ancestral line, similar to the concept of luck in contemporary thinking; however, its level can be raised and lowered by action and ritual, allowing a life of great deeds to grow ever more vital and mighty with each word and work. Hamingja is a complex and extremely Germanic idea that has few cognates with which it can be easily described. It is recommended that those interested in deepening their understanding of any of the aforementioned terms begin a thorough study to better approach the work at hand.

Sal is the binding force that brings all these pieces together and is loosened at the moment when the önd ceases to move within the lík.

THE INNER YGGDRASILL CONCEPT

An ash I know, Yggdrasil its name,
With water white is the great tree wet;
Thence come the dews that fall in the dales,
Green by Urð's well does it ever grow.

Völuspá, Bellows trans.

In many spiritual traditions, the cosmos is perceived as being a great tree that holds all of reality in its roots, trunk and branche, and the Northern European folkway is no exception. There are many written works that delve into lore of the World Tree in Norse cosmology, but we are concerned primarily with the ancient idea of the microcosm being a smaller, but generally identical version of the macrocosm. By following this poetic line of spiritual reasoning, we see Yggdrasill as a greater representation of the individual's physical/spiritual being.

In work with the staðas, different areas of the Yggdrasill complex can and should be focused on, and connections opened and repaired between them as energy alignment occurs through the course of the exercises. Practitioners of Kundalini yoga will be familiar with the idea of different areas of the spine and body representing specific process and ideas in the form of the chakras. From the Northern European perspective. these are seen as the "hvels," or "realms," and each has its own influence and function.

PLANT MODALITY

Another useful tool in our work of connecting the Self with the All, as it pertains to the concept of man as the World Tree is the idea of plant modality, an idea perhaps new to some practitioners of the Northern Way. During meditation, physical movement is ceased; the breathing slows to an almost non-existent rhythm; the heartbeat is reduced by vast measure; the outer senses are cut off, and the inner ones are controlled until they become silent. Man becomes tree — biological life, rooted in place physically, but no longer held within the stream of chaos and madness that characterizes the so-called "human condition."

THE DENIZENS OF YGGDRASILL
and their ESOTERIC MEANINGS

In the Eddas, we are told that there are certain denizens of the tree, beyond those who exist in their various realms. These dwellers contain depths of hidden meaning for the dedicated pursuant. At the heights of the Tree, we find an unnamed eagle, upon whose brow rests the hawk Veðrfolnir. On the outstretching branches, the four stags Dáinn, Dvalinn, Duneyr, and Durathrór. At the roots, Níðhöggr, and a brood of uncountable serpents gnawing at the foundations of the cosmos —and between the heights and the base, the squirrel Ratatoskr scurries, carrying messages and insults back and forth. At the northernmost edge of the cosmos, the eagle Hræsvelgr beats his massive wings and creates the universal winds that blow through the leaves of Lærað.

Looking deeper, we can glean much from these enigmatic symbols. The unnamed eagle at the top of the tree represents reason, and the highminded intellect. He sits at the peak of everything, surveying the rest of the cosmic geography with a piercing gaze, and counts himself the enemy of the writhing chaos that eats away at the tree's base. The hawk who perches on his brow is the equivalent of the ajna chakra or tilak in Hindu mysticism — spiritual sight that exists on an even higher plane than that of mundane perception — this bird's gaze sweeps through every facet of the universe, from root to branch, leaf to sap. If the eagle sees what is without, the hawk sees what is within everything, the Self in all aspects. He is representative of enlightenment, transcendence and revelatory vision. The stags who live among the branches devouring the leaves are physical vitality and balance — they feed on the overall health of leaf, branch and root, forming a symbiotic relationship with the tree: as they consume, they stimulate new growth. Ratatoskr runs entirety of the tree, acting as the circulatory system, both physically and spiritually — he alternates between chaos and ruin, structure and order, constantly on the move and connecting the two together. Hræsvelgr is the wind, the breath that flows through the cosmos, filling it with rhythmic life. Finally, Níðhöggr and the serpents at the roots are dissolution, entropy, ruin. They exist in all things ordered by cosmic law, and return all but the great Imperishable to chaos and death — with no power over the Unmoving, they impotently gnaw at the heart of Being forever. As one perceives the All, so he is — by looking this way at the tree and its dwellers, we can continue on our path to understanding the Self in All, and unite ourselves with the undying.

THE CENTRAL AXIS

"My breath, the cosmic winds;
My spine, the pillar of the universe—
My heart: the center of the world."

Asgarðr—
Residing at the top of the skull, the crown of existence, this realm is that of the highest being: elevated consciousness and ecstatic states far beyond the planes of thought and reason. Controlling the inspiration, and ruling the processes of the wild, divine madness. These upper two hvels correspond to Consciousness, Thought, Spirit, Ecstasy and Being.

Ljósálfheimr—
The seat of the intellect, the rational mind and the house of judgment and decisiveness, Ljósálfheimr can be related to the hugr and minni, the acts of thinking and remembering on a basic level. It is indicative of mental clarity, also, not of the clouded mind overcome with emotion, but the pure and crystalline realms of shining knowledge.

Miðgarðr—
There realm of :M: and the literal crossing of all worlds. Miðgarðr
stands in the center of the great weave of Wyrd, both changed by word
and action and changing the other worlds in turn. The vitki begins his
journey here: in potential. This is the central of what I call the Five
Realms of Becoming, those being Miðgarðr, Vanaheimr, Jötunheimr,
Niflheimr and Muspellsheimr- the realm: that correspond directly to
the Physical, the Emotional (direct), the Social. Existing on the
horizontal plane of being and becoming, rather than the vertical one of
spirituality and consciousness, these areas are those that are more
connected with the temporal, the transitory, and the perishable.
Miðgarðr is unique among them as representing the Self, existing at the
same time in both the areas of spirit and matter, perishable and
imperishable. It is only through the complete understanding of All that
the parts of the Self which are transitory can be removed.

Svartálfheimr—
From the deep places, the magician brings forth creation, lust, desire
and form. Located in the groin, this hvel controls the hamr and can be
felt to hold a great deal of might. It is this energy that can be utilized
by storing up sexual energy to be brought up the central axis and
converted into spiritual force. It is also the realm concerned with the
principles of power, fear, anxiety and control, and is associated strongly
with Hel as one of the two chthonic realms, the true Underworlds of
the soul.

Hel—
The dark, somber realms of the unconscious — if Svartálfheimr's
secrets reside in the often misunderstood area of the subconscious, then
Hel is certainly even "deeper." There is danger in being trapped and lost
in this sullen silence, but at the gnarled roots of the tree is
unimaginable strength. Hel deals primarily with the "unknown," those
parts of ourselves and our psyche that are rarely, if ever delved into by
any but the most serious students of the universe.

THE HORIZONTAL PLANE

Vanaheimr—
The rich, black earth of prosperous energy. Vanaheimr is the vitki's balancing point to all the forces of chaos, strain and madness; he can sink his feet into warm soil and understand the joys of growth, fruitfulness and holiness. This hvel corresponds with pleasure, love, connectedness and devotion.

Jötunheimr—
The wilds. Howling winds and encroaching chaos. This is entropy, not evil; here is represented tenacity on a cosmic level, an enduring force of constant opposition and destruction. Every vitki requires an understanding and use of the energy to be found here. Jötunheimr is also inherently connected to violence, aggression, opposition and resistance.

Muspellsheimr—
The burning spark of life and creation, and the final end of immolating flame. Here we have both opposition and unity, an important principle of universal understanding — a single idea that breeds many. Muspellsheimr is the primal fire of :F: the necessary quickening of matter, and the burning lust of constant generation. Correspondences include passion, creativity, instinctual action and sensuality.

Niflheimr—
The swirling rime of all-potential. Niflheimr is matter, waiting to be seeded and realized. A sea of possible thought and near-reality, here is where the vitki goes to grasp at unrealized destiny. Its primary elements can be associated with basic emotional impulse, primal idea formations and simple physical manufacturing. The rudimentary seeds that form in Niflheimr act together with hvels on the vertical axis to form unbelievably powerful processes — the work you are now looking act could be considered the working in tandem of Niflheimr, Muspellsheimr, Ljósálfheimr and Miðgarðr.

By understanding the primary rulerships of each hvel, or realm, we can focus on and master specific areas of our consciousness instead of swimming blindly about the whole, wondering idly to ourselves, "where did that thought come from," or "why did I dream of this or that," or "how can I possibly achieve this seemingly impossible feat?" We become travelers of our own cosmic model, able to run up and down our own central axis at will, binding the primal might of the horizontal hvels with the majestic fire of the vertical axis to perform and create things of legendary proportion. We transition our focus in the blink of an eye from the perishable and slaving to the infinite and sublime... we destroy the destroyable and become the eternal!

CHAPTER TWO:
BREATHING AND MEDITATION

Then from the throng did three come forth,
Mighty and gentle, from the home of the gods
Two without orlog on the land they found,
Askr and Embla, of little might.
Önd they had not, óðr they had not,
Heat nor motion, nor goodly hue;
Önd gave Óðinn, óðr gave Hoenir,
Heat gave Loðurr and goodly hue.

— Prophecy of the Seeress, author's trans.

The fiery energy that gives life to the lík, önd, is an integral part of beginning work with staðagaldr. With practiced application of öndwork, all parts of the soul complex can be purified, healed and given increased vitality. In the lore, it is the gift that Óðinn gives to the unfated Askr and Embla, the literal Fire of Life that permeates the body.

CONSCIOUS AND UNCONSCIOUS BREATHING

The first step of öndwork is to simply become aware of one's own breathing. Like many other unconscious processes, it is our tendency to ignore the very activities that give life to the body. By becoming aware of them, we can begin to understand how they affect us, and how they can be trained and utilized to alter the consciousness, add potency to the body and mind, and soothe the spirit.

This exercise should be practiced often and for increasing amounts of time, until one can easily slip into "awareness" of his breath. Seating oneself in the Valknutr position (see below) one should begin to inhale, slowly, through the nose, paying attention to the sound being made by the breath entering the windpipe and lungs. When the lungs are full (using the stomach and diaphragm to breathe, and not the chest) one should hold the breath for a few seconds, and then begin to slowly exhale until the breath is completely emptied — pushing the stomach toward the spine to completely expel all air. The entire process should be focused on, and should take anywhere from 12-20 seconds, although as one continues with their breathing exercises, this will increase dramatically. To start with, one should perform daily exercises to aid in breathing rhythmically, increasing the time between inhale and exhale with each breath. Extended practice of this will lead to natural rhythmic breathing without the need for focus, and this is the ideal goal of the exercise.

LAGUZ EXERCISE

Those having difficulty with the breathing exercises, or a hard time with the idea of "consciously breathing" can try the following exercise: lay on your back, with arms in the Laguz position. As the breath is drawn in, allow the arms to naturally raise in a straight line until they are above the head. When they are all the way extended, the lungs are full, and you can exhale, lowering your arms as you do so. This is a good way to "breathe with the whole body," and can be a beneficial :L: exercise in and of itself.

VALKNUTR BREATHING

This method of breathing focuses on opening the pathways of energy through the body that form the shape of the Valknutr, and using this form as a meditative guide throughout the process. The information included here is an abbreviated version of the original, which can be found in the pages of Gróandibók, the Galdragldi's apprentice work by Gandvaldr Bláskikkja.

The position taken is similar to the half-lotus yoga posture, as shown. Drawing in the breath with the diaphragm, through the nose, and down the vertical axis, into Svartálfheimr. From here, let the energy flow into the first triangle, made by the position of the legs. (The flow divides at the groin) As the energy permeates the lower triangle, it is then absorbed through the palms of the hands and passes into the tow upper triangles created by the arms and shoulders. It continues through Ljósálfheim in the throat, and descends downward again toward SA to complete the entire Valknutr. At this point the breath is held, and the force is used to awaken and charge the entire form from lower to higher regions. When the breath is ready to be expelled, the sustenance and might gained on the inhale is kept, while the unclean air and expended energy is expelled along the central column and out the mouth.

MEDITATION AND CLEANSING THE SACRED ENCLOSURE

There are a myriad of times when it becomes desirable for the vitki to cleanse the soul of all the things that may clutter it: stress, anxiety, anger, negative energy, emotions and so on. At this point, it should be noted that as one practices and moves towards the mastery of many of these tactics of rune work, that (while infinitely more easily done) there becomes no need to divide them from daily life, and that one may find oneself using these techniques and exercises in the middle of everyday situations. There is a great power in being able to tap into the methods, say, in the middle of a conversation, or a particularly stressful situation the individual might be facing at the time.

It is an unfortunate truth that man allows himself to be swept in every direction at any time by thought, whim and circumstance — swirling about like a splinter in a flood, constantly at the mercy of everything around him and within him. There comes a time when the individual must decide for himself whether he would be the cause or the affected, and begin to train the body and mind accordingly. Although there are many techniques that can be used to begin this, I have found one to be extremely effective, that being the ISA exercise outlined in the following paragraph.

The main desired effect of this form of meditation is to control those factors that attempt to distract one form his work — the two foremost ones being sense and the subconscious. Whether it be outside stimulation or internal chaos from the deep waters of thought and emotion, it can be exceedingly difficult at first to master them and stay the course. By using controlled breathing and vibration from vocalized runic forms, one can bring these to heel and sink into the undisturbed realms of deep meditation.

Begin by assuming either the Valknutr position or preferred variant, and close or half-close the relaxed eyes. Bring your breathing into rhythm in and out through the nose with slow inhalation and exhalation, being sure to keep the spine straight and aligned so that there are no blockages along the central axis. Once you have achieved this, deepen the breath further, and work to double the time spent on both the inhale and exhale, holding for a moment on fullness and emptiness. Contemplate nothing – when a thought arises, acknowledge it, then release it, without punishing yourself or becoming aggravated at the frequency with which they occur.

At this point, the body should be very relaxed and the breathing slowed to a great degree – now, with the same rhythm you have already developed, galdr the ISA root sound, that being the vowel seed of :I: (pronounced ee) Use this sound to drive everything out of your mind, your being, so that there is nothing left but the vibration.

Experience the utter contraction of the rune, as over time, even the vibration of the singing will seem to disappear and leave you in a true realm of stasis – silent, empty and complete. This should be continued for a long period of time, until the vitki truly feels and thinks nothing – no thought arises from within him, and no sensory experience is felt without; there is no longer a within and without, simply Being.

After reaching this point of the meditation and holding it until the desired end point, the galdr should stop, and be replaced with a threefold intonation of the :H: rune – the cosmic matrix from which all matter and being spring, and into that Eternal that even the universe dissolves. This method of emptying and purifying the entire Being is representative of universal death and rebirth on a miniature scale – the only difference between man and the cosmos is degree, not essence.

THE STRANDS OF WYRD

I know where Óðinn's eye is hidden,
Deep in the wide-famed well of Mímir;
Mead from the pledge of Óðinn each morn
Does Mímir drink: would you know yet more?

Völuspá, Bellows trans.

Another positive technique of meditation is using it as a way of tracing and visualizing the strands of one's Wyrd, in order to perceive the way they are woven, possible outcomes of past actions, and possible effects on the lives of others, and those lives effects on one's own. This sort of work, when done thoroughly and properly, can be much more effective than any other form of so called "divination."

One should begin this exercise simply, in the same fashion as the other meditation work discussed above, especially the ISA technique previously outlined. From an emptied and purified state, one can reach the disconnected point that he needs to, in order to view and dissect his actions and deeds in a practical and neutral way. After accomplishing the preliminary meditations, he should choose a single, seemingly innocuous action from the day's events, and exploration should begin with the following questions:

What were the events that led up to the action?
What was the action in reaction to (if anything)?
What did the action directly effect?
What was the immediate outcome of that effect?

These questions should be asked from a state of detachment, as though one were seeing them done by someone else. He should completely remove his personal biases and prejudices from the situation, and answer all of these queries honestly and completely. It is imperative that the vitki know himself thoroughly, and have no illusions or self-deceptions in place to cloud his mind from the truth.

From here, one should follow the weave further. What effect did the action have on those whose Wyrd was connected to those who witnessed it (obviously, one can only answer this question within reason, but extended practice of this exercise can develop of incredible accuracy.)? What influence or effect did the action have on those individuals who were not even directly involved, and so on. Like ripples on a pond, the vitki should begin from a very close perspective, and gradually work his way outward and outward, until he can see every possible effect and stirring in the great weave.

Orlög and wyrd are many layered subjects, and further study of these conceptions can aid the vitki in many ways.

CHAPTER THREE:
GALDR AND MANTRA

If it is understood that on one level the runes are representative of the universe itself, and are seed-forms of the great mysteries of our worlds, that thought must be traced to its root. The connection between runes, galdr and the principles of creation is an unmistakable one that cannot be overlooked by any seeker – to study and know the runes is an attempt to truly know the universe we live in, and a struggle to find not only our place in it, but everything else's place as well.

There are three main foundations for staðagaldr: physical position, through which we attempt to synthesize and gain a perfect understanding of a specific rune or runes; mental focus and spiritual intention, through which we give the forms meaning and depth, as we internalize them and grow from our experience and applied practice; and finally, the breath and sound that we bring together to create vibration and manifest change.

The word galdr comes from a root word meaning "to sing or to chant," but is in the ON almost always used in context referring to a cham or spell, and became synonymous later on with anything related to the esoteric – the vocal idea of which translates over beautifully to rune-work, as the etymology of this word "rune" can be traced to the PIE word reu – means "to whisper" and "to roar." Ultimately, the word is first found in 4th century Gothic as runa, meaning "mystery" or "secret". This vibratory and vocal idea permeates the fabric of Norse myth, beginning with the creation itself. As sparks from Muspellsheimr and ice from Niflheimr come together in the great charged space of Ginnungagap, a form takes shape, which is called Ymir. The word Ymir comes from an ON root literally meaning "roarer", or "roaring one," and form this great, primal representation of matter, force, vitality and wild potential, the realms are shaped by Oðinn, and his two brothers Vili and Vé, in an act of sacrificial patricide. Just like knowing the root meaning of Ymir, it is helpful to know that the three brothers who utilize this primal force to create, Oðinn, Vili and Vé, would translate approximately into our language as "Ectasy, Will and Holiness."

From this ancient birth of the realm we (usually) exist in, we see matter being willfully formed and shaped from a roaring energy, a vibratory and vocal quality that continues to appear later in the mythology.

The main point to note here is that the roaring by itself forms matter, and transforms the environs around it in a seemingly random, haphazard sort of way, but it is only through ecstatic, inspired energy, will, and sacrality, or wholeness, that a conscious forming and directed creative process is able to take place. This idea carries over to rune work and staðagaldr directly, in that the rune-forms and sounds by themselves are merely representations – references if you will, to act as a jumping off point for us, as seed from which we can learn, transform, grow, used to alter, shape and influence our realities.

The correlation between vocalization and the runes continues when we look later on in the myths to the point where Oðinn is hanging from the World Tree's branches, wounded by spear, and offered to himself in a ritualized sacrifice involving sensory deprivation, pain and fatigue – he peers down into the great depths after hanging there for nine nights, and takes up the runes, the mysteries, the understanding of the universe – and the next verse reiterates this with the famous words "oepandi nam", or "screaming I took them". With great roar, Oðinn takes up the mysteries of the worlds, and with that fortuitous vocalization, his understanding dawns, and he falls back from there.

While we attempt to experience this same level of enlightenment, we use the vocal, spiritual and physical forms of the runes as a way of focusing our energies on them, experiencing them fully by immersing ourselves in the stave forms, the lore, our personal interpretations and understanding of them, the vibratory qualities of their sound the physical postures that represent them and the effect that all this has on us, the world around us, and the worlds within us. We use it to bear, choosing specific runes to embody certain principles and thought-forms, and giving them life through sound and sense, – bringing them from the realm of all– potential into the realm of actual being. Each time we perform this act, we are recreating the holy process of the three brothers, using the roaring, Ymir, to shape and alter their surroundings, their perceptions and their understanding of reality in the way they chose.

GALDR TECHNIQUE

With rune galdr, there is no real wrong or right way to go about it. There are as many ways to intone the runes as there are ways to perceive them, and one's own tried and true methods are always the best for the individual. The following are two exercises: the first being a basic Staðagaldr working to awaken the central axis and connect the energies along the vertical pathways, and the second is one of the author's creation. These are intended both for personal use and as an example of some ways that the vitki can approach the various aspects and layers of their own work.

AWAKENING THE CENTRAL AXIS

The principle behind this working is to focus on each of the five hvels that make up the vertical pathway of the body, and galdr the corresponding runic vowel forms to awaken and charge each one in turn. It should be performed slowly, with deep contemplation on each hvel as the staða is assumed and the rune galdred, and special attention should be given to the pathways between each hvel – what sensations or perceptions does the vitki experience at each of the five hvels? How does the runic vibration affect these sensations? What, if anything, feels out of place or disjointed along the way? For more advanced practice, how can one implement different runic energies into these realms and pathways? These are the sort of questions the vitki should be asking himself at every turn, in every different area of his rune work.

The working is begun with a deep breath of cleansing fire, drawing that pure holy might into every area of his being and holding its burning flame inside, consuming the dross. On exhalation, nothing remains of the detritus – all is new and bright.

The :U: staða is assumed, and the vitki galdrs the runic sound into the deeps of Hel. The work continues by moving through the vowel forms in order, :A: for Asgarðr, :I: for Svartálfheimr, :E: for Ljósálfheim and :O: for Miðgarðr.

Herjan Galdr:

Beginning with a long, slow breath inward, the beginning intonation of :H: and :E: is begun. The cleansing breath is in itself a meditation on the gift of önd, the breath of fire, given to Askr and Embla by the High One when they were as yet unfated. These initial rune-sounds are also meaningful: :H: begins a creative process, a seed of germination in the realm of Ljósálfheim, deep within the chest, here represented by :E: – an unstoppable for rising upwards, as the sound moves vertically through the core and its vibrations begin the chain of functionality embodied within the galdr. The chest and throat contract to form the first part of this longer piece, a fettering, as the vitki binds himself to the task at hand and gives over this entire process to this one endeavor...

...as the :R: :J: sound is transitioned to, the fetters are burst, the throat opens and the primal force of creation pours forth. Movement continues up through the higher areas of the chest and throat, moving toward the face and crown of the head. Warmth and vibration spread throughout the entire body, as the vitki's consciousness elevates towards the ecstatic. When the :A: rune is intoned, the volume and pitch of the galdr is increased, and the óðr is unleashed as an opening, liberating, opposition-destroying wave that emanates from the forehead and spreads outward, enveloping the entire Yggdrasill complex in its potent might. This element of the process is its most precious –a manifestation of Óðroerir, the great stirrer of inspiration– within the grasp of its wondrous drops, the vitki truly has the opportunity to experience the actual rune of Ansuz. Finally, the :N: acts as a grounding vibration, felt properly in the face and nasal areas, as the vitki once again returns to his state of normal consciousness; the seat of the intellect and reason, the Thought and the Mindfulness, coming back to rest once again on the shoulders of the Way-tame wanderer.

RUNIC MANTRAS

There are many runic formulae that have been discovered on various stones, bracteates, amulets and the like, and each of them can be studied and utilized in run-galdr, as well as formulas of one's own design – in order to fully understand and craft one's own runic formula for use in galdr, there are some basic principles to keep in mind: Throughout the runic ætts, we see that in each ætt, there are two vowel forms, each of which represents a core element or property, that can be combined with the more wide and expansive consonant seeds to form complex and layered formula, or working words. Through continued study and application, there are essentially limitless combinations and principles that can be used to empower and deepen our practice.

When creating these formulae, we can look to some historical ones for a better understanding of how this can be done most effectively. As an example of how this functions we will look at the :luwatuwa: formula, originally found on the Vadstena bracteates discovered in 1744. The translation of this word is generally taken to be "to the earth, to the sky," but deeper meanings can be plumbed when we look at its qualities in vocalized galdr. When sung in a repetitive manner, new words form themselves in and around the root-word, a deliberate tool which can be seen in other runic formulas such as :lathu: as well as other IE sources in general. (For example, scholars of the Bhagavad Gita have stated that the best way to understand the Gita is to simply vocalize the word over and over, until natural rhythm turns the word into "Tagi," which means "one who has renounced everything for God.") Using this technique within the luwatuwa framework, we can hear a vocal shift in between repetitions, forming a secondary mantra, in this case, the popularly inscribed "ALU", within this greater principle. Beside this we can see that there is generally a consonant/vowel/consonant/vowel format, or vice versa, rather than stacking multiple consonants or vowels in a row (although this is not always the case). Due to this, we can break down the meaning of a formula even more. For example, many are familiar with the Gebo Auja bindrune – combining the two runes :GA:::A: together for a meaning of "luck or gift from the gods," On helmets and spears have been found the inscription G A G A G A. We can probably surmise that the formula is not intended to be taken as the word Gagaga, but rather as a formulaic representation of the words Gebo Auja, sort of a runic acronym, if you will. By layering meaning upon meaning in this fashion, and secret upon secret, we are able to use the runes as a sort of mystical kenning tool – hiding the obvious in plain sight, there to read and understand only for those that truly know.

CHAPTER FOUR: STADAS

Fehu—
This position is formed utilizing a method I refer to as "Grasping the Spear." The hands are outstretched and placed one over the other in a vertical profile as though gripping the hilt of a spear. When performing this staða, one should keep the O.E. rune poem in mind: "Wealth is a comfort to all men, yet every man must give freely if he wants his lot of judgment from the lord." One is letting energy flow freely into and away from himself – there is no hoarding or storing up of energy here, simply receiving and giving in the same moment. It can be helpful to use the breathing exercises previously outlined, as one breathes in the fire of :F: and releases the used up energies throughout the lik.

Uruz—

Forming the rune by placing the hands flat against the earth and keeping the legs straight, one is rooted to the lower realms directly in two places at once. This forms a sort of electrical current in which the lík acts as the conducting agent for the strengthening flow of :U:. The lík is purified, empowered and healed by this wholesome might, and the will is rejuvenated. Singing the rune galdr during this staða is especially effective in the lower rages.

Thurisaz—
A posture visually indicative of directed force and sending. This
staða is one of focusing, transformation and harnessed will being
summoned and sent forth with purpose. The vitki is literally
drawing his might into the core and transforming it by an act of
the will to suit his need, so that it can be brought to bear
throughout the nine worlds, up and down the central axis of
Yggdrasill.

Ansuz—
    The second position in the elder runes utilizing the spear-gripping hand posture. Ansuz is the rune indicative of not only that Spear's owner, but of the ordeal he underwent and the great sacrifice made for the highest of rewards. The experience on the Tree was a death and rebirth into a new form of being: a mode of non-conditioned existence. It is these mysteries that are to be contemplated as the vitki undergoes his own Ordeal. Ansuz flows from the crown, the highest point, and can be used in conjunction with the HERJAN galdr to assist in raising the vitki from mere consciousness to something much greater.

Raiðo—

A dynamic posture designed to embody the principles of perpetual motion and right action. Stretching outward across the horizontal plane of being and becoming, the vitki removes himself from the great weave and sets his own course. The position can be alternated and should be struck with the strength and confidence of one who has his own hand on the tiller of destiny.

Kenaz—
     The vitki forms the staða for :K: and holds in his hands
the torches of illumination and highmindedness. Coupled with
the galdr that first contracts and the expands with the potent
force of inspiration and passion, this posture can be very useful
for striking the spark that leads to the Fire.

Gebo—

A physical form of sacrifice and giving. The mysteries and truths of reciprocal exchange resonate strongly here... the streams of force that intersect one another should be carefully noted and the place where they cross paid attention to especially when one is exploring the :g: staða.

Wunjo—
        Pressing the palms together, raising the arms and
placing them against the forehead in a symbol of wellbeing,
gratitude and blessing is a good start to begin contemplating and
working with the particular energies associated with this rune.
Wunjo is less of a striving and more of a being... instead of
dissatisfaction and stress, it can be utilized to change the
perception and bring about a calm satisfaction, or a profound
feeling of even harmoniousness. Rather that the wild ecstasies of
:a: that can leave one feeling drained and "down", :w: focuses on
a constant peace that does not fluctuate or dissipate.

Hagalaz—

       Using the younger stave form for the rune, the vitki literally reaches into all worlds at once – visualizing the internal Yggdrasill complex, one can see the four outer realms of the manifesting plane: Niflheimr to the north, Jötunheimr to the east, Muspellsheimr to the south and Vanaheimr to the west. The vitki is no longer just a part of the universe, rather, he becomes it: the seed of creation, the complex form of the ever changing universe. He is the Unmoving Mover. From here, one can sink from the deepest depths and ascend to the greatest heights, creating roads and rivers between each of the nine worlds. This is an especially appropriate staða for work involving the sending of runic energies into specific areas of the World Tree. While performing the :H: staða, the idea is to create a fluidity of motion expressing the ever-flowing thought of the cosmos writ large. The accompanying photo demonstrates one way that this can be accomplished, but the practitioner is encouraged to purposefully explore further methods and approaches.

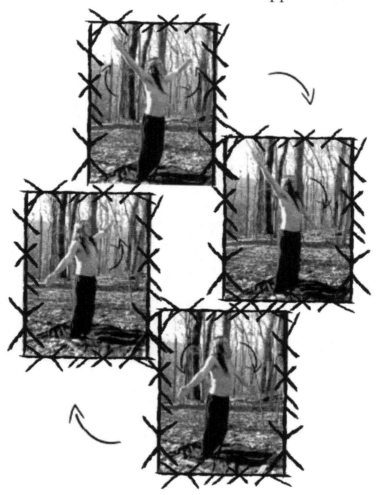

Nauðiz—
          Considering the rune poems associated with it, Nauðiz emerges as a staða of friction and preparation. It draws down energy from above and forms an intersecting point in the core where the heat and power of the Inner Fire can be kindled and sustained. As a rune of sexual energy, it pertains to the idea of generating that potency without expending it, but rather transforming it into spiritual force – storing up that fuel for the Winter.

Isa—

The form of supreme stillness. Perfect and concentrated, a pure form from the heart of Niflheimr, the realm of all-potential. From this place of silence and focus, anything becomes possible – when the power of this rune stills and quiets all other processes, one is limitless and without form, free to move beyond the bounds of reason or intellect. Conversely, it can be used as the ultimate contractor – bringing all thought and matter together into nothingness. Its benefits on personal meditation cannot be overemphasized.

Jera/Ár—

Using the younger stave form, this staða can be utilized to meditate on the beautiful nature of harvest and plenty, especially as it pertains to sowing the seeds of the great work and reaping the benefit and reward of them in time. The lines from Sigrdrífumál "Hail Earth who gives to all," is a fitting meditational tool for this staða, and one might also consider the vertical runic binding of :A::J::M:: as a source of wisdom and contemplation.

Eihwaz—

Forming oneself into the vertical axis of the world tree and stretching out branches and roots, the vitki can himself branch out his awareness into all thing that the mighty Yew holds. A runic mystery of initiation, austerity and awakening, the :EI: posture is full of potential for one who has the dedication and will to endure.

Perthro—
Even the form itself lowers one towards the deep places where
the great Well lies. Beneath the roots of the tree, meditation can
commence on the unbreakable laws of the universe, órlög and
Wyrd.

Elhaz/Algiz—

      Stretching upwards, the vitki forms a connection point with the realms above. Sending and receiving energy at the same time, one exists rooted to the earth with his hands in the heavens. This form is also useful for warding the vitki from any sort of negative energies he may be experiencing, as it purifies through association with the upper realms of consciousness.

Sowilo—
A salute to the life giving force of Sun's rays — the bright light of victory, overcoming of obstacle and melting the ice of stasis. The Sowilo form is one of absorption and renewal.

Tiwaz—

A master-rune, and one that never breaks faith with princes. Tiwaz's simple form belies its massive complexity as a rune of life and death, sacrifice and consequence, form and void. It's upward pointing stave form is an important facet of physical work with it, in that contemplation on the corresponding charm from Hávamál can lead one from Hel to Asgarðr.

Berkano—
Growing, being, becoming, fading away and being reborn. During one's work with the :B: form, they may experience all these conditions of being, and in so doing, focus on the mystery of transcending these states entirely.

Ehwaz—
    Opening the pathways within the trunk and riding forth, the vitki can use this staða as his spiritual mount to traverse the unknown roads between the realms. Also effective when used in conjunction with meditation on the fetch-spirit, or faring forth in this modality.

Mannaz—
Man in potential. A position for intense contemplation on one's place in the universe, the Self, his (dis)connection with those things around him and movement beyond the boundaries of his humanity. We are not the body, just as the driver is not the vehicle. This is not to say that the physical form is not sacred, but that we are not connected to it beyond its use as a housing. When we can see past this, we become free to move about without physical limitation and realize higher forms of being as :M:

Laguz—

A flowing rune that can be used to good effect in breathing exercises both standing and lying down. Might from one's blood and energy alignment is personified and can be tapped into with this form, envisioned as a smoothly moving waterfall. The Laguz rune is also one of exploration of our deeper psyche, allowing for a deeper knowledge of what lies beneath the surface.

Ingwaz—
        The womb, fruitfulness, fertility and new growth — the physical form of :NG: is an obvious reference to its properties and function.

Othala—

    A firm connection with the ideas of ancestry, centering might, Miðgarðr. As the Self is the center of all things, so the individual is the center of his own world. By breaking down the barriers between "this" and "that" we do not lose our Selves, we gain the All!

Dagaz—
Dusk and dawning, Sun and Moon, light and darkness, in between times and balance. The position of Dagaz forms a dividing point on the physical body. This deliberate reminder should put one in mind of the paradox in everything, and the principle that opposites are not so at all, merely two perspectives of the Same: just as either side of a coin is still the same coin.

CHAPTER FIVE:
BINDRUNES AND ADDITIONAL STADAS

With a few notable exceptions, I have seen very little effort to work with the Elder Futhark staðas to make them more natural, practical and useful to the practitioner, let alone development of more advanced staðas and non-runic positions. Similar to the principle of music being written for instruments by composers who do not, in fact, play those instruments – often times, the way the piece is transcribed is exceedingly clumsy or difficult to work with those approaching it from the angle of player instead of theorist.

This is something I have seen far too often in the field of esoteric literature — the bulk of written work being published by those who are skilled at intellectual theorizing but have little or no experience putting those ideas into passionate action. Even those more famous names in the area of "esoteric runology", although credit must go to them for their work and inspiring words on the subject, have fallen into this morass of word over work — going so far as to claim that they "have gone beyond the need for ritual, practice and applied rune work."

For my part, I do not believe that there is such a point, even for the most developed and way-wise vitkar. Constant discipline, practice and application are required for those who would keep their feet on the rough path to Understanding — we have chosen a Road With No End, subjecting ourselves to constant Ordeal and sacrifice. At every moment of dawning realization, the entire process begins again, as the very nature of the runes is to constantly move beyond us, beckoning us ever onwards toward the great reward of the Self.

The previous text is a brief look at some of the developing work I have undertaken in the past year – my reason for producing it is to inspire action from those who are hungry, ravenous and filled with the Need to re-invent, adapt, discover and re-discover. Those familiar with traditional asanas in the school of Hatha yoga may find that continued practice and exploration of that direction proves increasingly beneficial when placed in a context more fitting to the mindset that produced them – time has a way of diluting and diverting even the strongest of rivers. The deliberate intention is not to "steal" from existing Indo European system, but to bring them into view and use in a form that resonates with the Germanic soul and ancestral calling.

Their usefulness and effectiveness when taken "as is" remains unquestionable – however, the format need only be altered and developed in an organic fashion for the entire system to roar and surge with the natural power of the Germanic blood. It is my suggestion and current ongoing work to bring the ancient systems and schools of yoga back to where they belong, instead of leaving them the province of a folk who have become something far removed from where they began.

On Magic:

A No-Bullshit Primer on Working the Will
by Paul Waggener

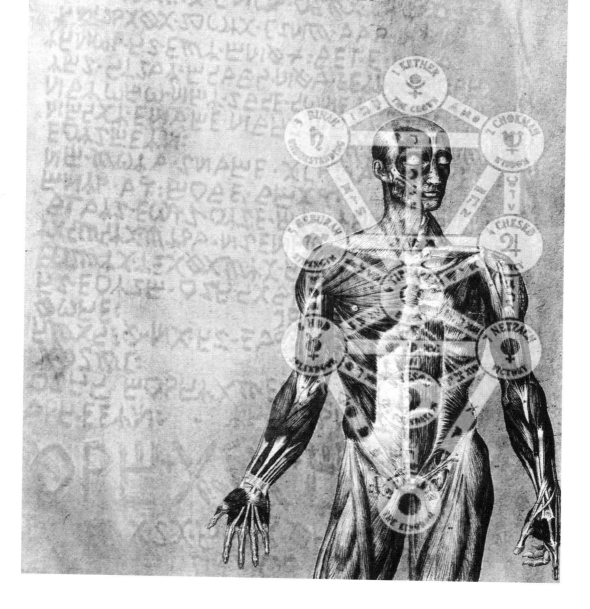

I'M GOING TO SPARE YOU THE USUAL TYPE OF OBLIGATORY INTRODUC-
TION MOST OF THESE THINGS HAVE, THAT OUTLINE WHAT SECRET ORDER
I'M A MEMBER OF, WHAT MY MADE-UP RANK IS, AND WHAT COSMIC SECRETS
I HAVE THAT YOU HAVE TO BECOME A MEMBER TO LEARN. I ASSUME, IF
YOU'RE STILL READING THIS AFTER SEEING THE TITLE, YOU KNOW THAT
THIS WON'T BE THAT KIND OF WORK.

ALTHOUGH IT'S TRUE THAT I HAVE, IN FACT, BEEN A MEMBER OF MANY OF
THE AFOREMENTIONED SECRET ORDERS, AND HAVE ATTAINED MANY
MADE-UP RANKS IN THEM, AND HAVE EVEN WORKED MY WAY TO THE TOP
LEADERSHIP ROLE IN MORE THAN ONE- I HAVE FOUND MOST OF THEM TO
BE A WASTE OF TIME. NOT JUST MY OWN, BUT THOSE WHO LOOKED TO
JOIN THEM AS WELL. WHAT MOST OF THESE ORDERS HAVE IN COMMON IS A
TOP DOWN HIERARCHY (BASED ALMOST ENTIRELY ON INTERNAL POLITICS),
IN WHICH INFORMATION IS DISSEMINATED AT A RATE THAT THE "MASTERS"
FEEL IS APPROPRIATE FOR THE "STUDENTS."

"I've never been one for authority."

I'VE NEVER BEEN ONE FOR AUTHORITY. I'VE ALSO UNDERSTOOD THAT
THESE GROUPS WOULD BE UNLIKELY TO SURVIVE IF THEY SIMPLY PRE-
SENTED ALL THE INFORMATION THEY'VE ACQUIRED, WITHOUT AT-
TEMPTING TO HOLD ONTO THESE LITTLE "SECRETS" AND "FORBIDDEN
RITUALS," BECAUSE THEN THE GROUP WOULD BE BASED AROUND
ACTUAL PRACTICE AND LEARNING, ON AN EVEN KEEL, WITH THE MORE
KNOWLEDGEABLE LOOKING TO AID THOSE WITH LESS, IN A FREE EX-
CHANGE OF IDEAS. NONE OF THE USUAL SUSPECTS WOULD DREAM OF
SUCH A THING.

IT IS MY OPINION THAT ALL MAGICAL PRACTICE IS BASED ON THE SAME BASIC FRAMEWORK, AND THAT IT IS ACTUALLY VERY SIMPLE, VERY BEAUTIFUL, AND VERY FUNCTIONAL IF YOU PUT IN THE TIME AND DEDICATION TO TREAT IT LIKE ANY OTHER SERIOUS ENDEAVOR IN YOUR LIFE. IT'S AMAZING THE AMOUNT OF PEOPLE OUT THERE WHO THINK THEY'RE ENTITLED TO IMMEDIATE RESULTS IN THIS FIELD- THEY'RE USUALLY THE SAME ONES WHO QUIT EVERY FITNESS PROGRAM THEY'VE EVER STARTED, NEVER REALLY LEARNED HOW TO PLAY THAT GUITAR IN THEIR ROOM, HAVE A HUNDRED HALF FINISHED NOVELS ON THEIR COMPUTER, JUMP AROUND ON FAD DIETS, AND SHOW LITTLE CONSISTENCY IN ANY OF THEIR CHOSEN AREAS.

IT CANNOT BE STRESSED ENOUGH: WHAT WE SEE IN "PRACTICAL MAGIC" (A FUNNY TERM, BUT AN ACCURATE ONE IF YOU'RE NOT DELUSIONAL) IS A SERIES OF PRACTICES THAT ARE ACTUALLY MOSTLY BACKED BY MODERN SCIENCE, BUT THAT FORM A FRAMEWORK OF IDEAS AND INTERCONNECTED PROCESSES THAT HAVE TO BE DESCRIBED BY A CATCH ALL WORD THAT BRINGS THEM TOGETHER UNDER ONE ROOF; IT IS THOSE PRACTICES WE WILL BE DISCUSSING HERE.

We'll get right down to business, because I assume

you're reading this to learn something about magic.

FIRST, WE'RE GONNA TALK ABOUT THAT FUCKING HOKEY, BULLSHIT WORD, AND HOW MUCH I DON'T LIKE TO USE IT. THE WORD CONJURES UP IMAGES OF WIZARDS IN POINTED HATS SENDING WEEPING LITTLE PEOPLE ON ADVENTURES; OF WEIRDOS (AND NOT THE GOOD KIND) WHO ARE LIVING IN A DELUSIONAL FANTASY WORLD (AND ALSO THEIR MOTHER'S BASEMENT) IN WHICH THEY HAVE SOME KIND OF VAGUE "POWERS" THAT THEY NOT ONLY CAN'T REALLY DEFINE, BUT CERTAINLY CANNOT REPLICATE ON DEMAND.

IT IS A SHITTY WORD, THAT HAS TOO MANY CONNOTATIONS TO TRULY BE EFFECTIVE ANYMORE. THAT BEING SAID, I DON'T KNOW ANOTHER WORD THAT ACCURATELY DESCRIBES WHAT WE'RE TALKING ABOUT, SO I'M JUST GOING TO KEEP ON USING IT, IN THE WAY THAT CROWLEY DEFINED IT-

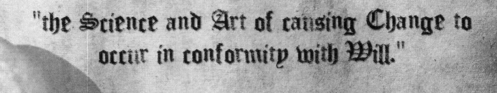

"the Science and Art of causing Change to occur in conformity with Will."

IT COULD BE ARGUED THAT EVERY ACTION IS CREATING CHANGE TO OCCUR IN CONFORMITY WITH THE WILL, BUT YOU'LL NOTICE THAT OLD A.C. CAPITALIZED THIS WORD, BECAUSE HE DIDN'T MEAN "DESIRE" OR "WANT," AS MANY USE THE TERM, HE MEANT "WILL," WHICH IS MORE LIKE "ONE'S TRUE DESTINY."

DISCOVERING THAT WILL, THAT HIGHER GOAL, WAS A BIG PART OF
WHAT CROWLEY'S ENTIRE METHOD WAS ABOUT (INTERESTED PARTIES
WHO ARE NOT FAMILIAR WITH MR. CROWLEY'S WORK CAN GET STARTED
WITH HIS "BOOK 4," AN EXCELLENT WORK FROM WHICH MUCH INSPIRA-
TION CAN BE TAKEN, AND FROM WHICH MUCH CAN BE IGNORED!) FOR
THE OBVIOUS REASON THAT, IF WE DON'T HAVE A GOAL, ANY ACTION
WILL ESSENTIALLY BE TREADING WATER- A WASTE OF OUR ENERGIES.

THIS IS THE FIRST TAKE-AWAY POINT: IN ALL AREAS OF LIFE, WE MUST
HAVE A DEFINED GOAL. FROM THERE, ANY ACTION TAKEN THAT IS NOT
MOTION TOWARD THAT HIGHER GOAL, THAT TRUE WILL, IS A BETRAYAL
OF SELF.

SO, LETS GET BACK TO IT- WHEN WE CALL MAGIC A "SCIENCE" AS WELL AS
AN "ART," THESE TWO THINGS SEEM TO CONTRADICT ONE ANOTHER, AS
ART IS AN EXPRESSION OF CREATIVITY, PASSION, INNER FIRE; SCIENCE IS
COLD, CLINICAL, RATIONAL. LIKE MANY THINGS, THIS SEEMING CON-
TRADICTION IS IN FACT COMPLETELY CONSONANT. IN ORDER TO EXCEL
AT ANY ART, WE MUST BE ABLE TO CAST A MERCILESS GAZE UPON IT, TO
BURN AWAY SELF-DELUSION, TO STUDY DATA AND RESULT, TO REMOVE
WISHFUL THINKING FROM OUR PRAXIS.

"In all areas of life, we must have a defined goal."

IF MAGIC IS A SCIENCE, ALBEIT AN UNPROVEN ONE (THERE ARE NOW
MANY SCIENTIFIC NAMES FOR PROCESSES THAT BEGAN AS UNPROVEN
IDEAS THAT FELL WITHIN THE ESOTERIC REALMS- ONE CAN LOOK AT THE
THEORY OF QUANTUM ENTANGLEMENT FOR A MIND-BENDING EXAMPLE
OF THIS), IT MUST BE PRACTICED ACCORDINGLY.

MUCH LIKE WEIGHTLIFTING, MUSICIANSHIP, PAINTING, AND SO ON- THE
PRACTICE COMES FROM A PASSION FOR IT, BUT THE WORK MUST BE RA-
TIONAL. IT MUST CREATE RESULTS THAT WE ARE CAPABLE OF REPRODUC-
ING, IMPROVING, AND FACILITATE PROGRESS FORWARD IN EVERY AREA
OF OUR LIFE.

THE SUCCESSFUL MAGICIAN IS SUCCESSFUL IN
ALL REALMS OF EXISTENCE- PHYSICAL, FINAN-
CIAL, MENTAL, SPIRITUAL. HE IS NOT SOME
BASEMENT DWELLING, SOCIALLY AWKWARD
WEAKLING, FRUSTRATEDLY LIVING OUT HIS EX-
ISTENCE IN SELF DELUSION, BUT RATHER- HE IS
CAPABLE, SOCIALLY ADEPT, SELF-CONTROLLED,
PHYSICALLY FIT- HE MAKES THE ABSOLUTE BEST
OUT OF ALL THE CARDS HE HAS BEEN DEALT IN
THIS LIFE, NOT CONTENT TO "SETTLE."

BEING A MAGICIAN IS NOT ABOUT ACCEP-
TANCE- IT IS ABOUT BREAKING RULES AND BAR-
RIERS, QUESTIONING THE NATURE OF EVERY-
THING, INCREASING THE WILL, BRINGING
THAT WILL TO BEAR ON SITUATIONS AND AL-
TERING THEM IN ACCORDANCE WITH THE
QUESTIONS "WHAT WOULD I CHANGE, AND
WHY, AND HOW?"

"Being a magician is not about acceptance- it is about breaking rules and barriers..."

THE DRIVING FORCE BEHIND THE
STUDY OF MAGIC IS LOGIC, DESPITE
HOW IT SEEMS TO ITS DETRACTORS-
LOOKING AT THE UNIVERSE AND SAYING
"IF THIS THING IS LIKE THIS, THEN THIS
LARGER MYSTERY IS LIKELY TO FOLLOW
SUIT," OR, AS WORDED BY THE FAMED
EMERALD TABLET OF HERMES TRIS-
MEGISTUS, "AS ABOVE, SO BELOW." THIS IS
NOT SOME NEO-PAGAN, HIPPIE STATE-
MENT OF "ALL IS ONE," BUT A SCIENTIFIC
LOGIC THAT LOOKS AT AN ATOM AND
SAYS "THE CELL LIKELY FOLLOWS SUIT.
THEN THE MAN, THEN THE PLANET,
THEN THE COSMOS."

PHYSICISTS ARE CURRENTLY HAVING DIFFICULTY WITH CERTAIN IDEAS NOT MAKING SENSE ON A MATHEMATICAL LEVEL IN CONJUNCTION WITH EACH OTHER, THAT IS TO SAY, ONE CAN ONLY EXIST IF THE OTHER IS RULED OUT, WHEREAS A MAGICAL THOUGHT PROCESS UNDERSTANDS THAT THINGS ARE LAYERED. THEY EXIST IN A STATE OF LOGIC AND DIS-LOGIC AT ONCE, BEING ONE THING, AND THEN ANOTHER THING AT THE SAME TIME, AND IN ORDER TO UNDERSTAND THEM, WE CANNOT SEPARATE THEM COMPLETELY INTO LOGIC, BUT HAVE TO LOOK AT THE "THING-NESS" OF THEM ALL AT ONCE.

TO PUT THIS ANOTHER WAY, IF ONE IS WORKING WITH RUNE GALDR, A FORM OF MAGICAL WORK THAT USES THE QUALITIES OF THE RUNES- (A GERMANIC MAGICAL ALPHABET, ESSENTIALLY A PERIODIC TABLE OF SPIRITUAL PROPERTIES) THEIR SHAPES, SOUNDS, AND PRINCIPLES TO ATTAIN AN EFFECT, AND IS SIMPLY INTONING THE ONE OF THE RUNE NAMES AND HOPING FOR AN EFFECT, HE HAS NOT UNDERSTOOD THE CORRECT USE. HE IS ONLY TAKING ONE BASE ASPECT OF THE RUNE, AND ATTEMPTING TO FATHOM IT THAT WAY. HE HAS TO INTERNALIZE AND GIVE THE IDEA LIFE THROUGH EXPERIENCING IT, BY DIGGING HIMSELF DEEP INTO LIFE'S BLOODY INNARDS AND GRASPING THOSE WILD MYSTERIES THAT ARE CONTAINED WITHIN EACH SEED-FORM THAT IS A RUNE.

SO HOW DOES IT ALL WORK? AS SOMEONE WHO HAS PRACTICED MAGIC WITHIN MANY DIFFERENT "SYSTEMS" (THAT IS TO SAY, DIFFERENT WORDINGS OF THE SAME BASIC IDEA) OVER THE COURSE OF MANY YEARS, I HAVE TO SAY THAT THEY ARE ALL OF THEM FILLED WITH SO MUCH BULLSHIT AND NEEDLESS "MYSTERIOSO" AS TO BE LARGELY IN-TOLERABLE AND USELESS TO THE SEEKER. ONE CAN ARGUE THAT MUCH OF WHAT IS THERE IS DELIBERATELY MADE CONFUSING AND INSCRUTA-BLE IN ORDER TO DRIVE THE SEEKER TO DEEPER DISCOVERY, AND TO A DEGREE, THERE IS SOME VALUE IN THIS. HOWEVER, THE ACTUAL PRO-CESSES AND IDEAS BEHIND THESE SYSTEMS ARE USUALLY THE SAME AT THE END OF THE DAY, AND I HAVE LITTLE IN THE WAY OF RESPECT OR PATIENCE FOR GROUPS OF AGING, OVERWEIGHT, SELF-IMPORTANT AND SELF-AGGRANDIZED "ADEPTS" WHO HAVE MANY TITLES AND ACCO-LADES WITHIN THEIR ORGANIZATION AND VERY LITTLE TO SHOW FOR IT OUT IN THE WORLD AT LARGE.

THE WAY TO WORK SIMPLE AND EFFECTIVE MAGIC IS THE SAME AS THE WAY TO WORK SIMPLY AND EFFECTIVELY IN ANY AREA:

KNOW YOUR GOAL.

PRACTICE OFTEN WITH THE TOOLS AT YOUR DISPOSAL. BE CONSISTENT IN THAT PRACTICE.

THE TOOLS OF THIS TRADE ARE THE RITUAL APPLICATION OF VISUALIZATION, SYMBOLISM, AND THE VOCALIZATION OF THE WILL.

Visualization

THE VERY FACT THAT OUR BRAINS ARE
CAPABLE OF CREATING IMAGERY AND
RE-CREATING THE PERCEPTUAL EXPERIENCES
ACROSS ALL THE SENSES, AND ALTERING
THEM, RE-FORMING THEM AND SO ON IS A
WONDROUS THING IN AND OF ITSELF, AND
SOMETHING WE PROBABLY ALL LOSE SIGHT
OF FROM TIME TO TIME.

EVERY SONG, EVERY PIECE OF ART, EVERY
BUILDING, EVERY CIVILIZATION WAS THE
PRODUCT OF CREATIVE VISUALIZATION.
TAKING MATERIAL FROM SOME VAGUE PLACE
WITHIN THE MIND/SPIRIT AND MOLDING IT
INTO SOMETHING, THEN BRINGING THAT
SOMETHING FROM THE WORLD OF THINGS
IN POTENTIAL, ACROSS THE BORDERS INTO
THE WORLD OF THINGS IN REALITY- FROM
THERE, THAT THING CAN AFFECT EVERY
OTHER BEING THAT COMES INTO CONTACT
WITH IT. IMAGINE: A MUSICIAN SNATCHES
THE IDEA FOR A SONG FROM THE ETHER, HE
SHAPES IT, MOLDS IT INTO POTENTIAL, THEN
CREATES IT THROUGH VIBRATION INTO A
REPRODUCIBLE THING THAT CREATES A SIM-
ILAR EMOTION IN ALL THAT HEAR IT,
AFFECTING THE VERY WAY THEY FEEL AT THE
TIME THEY HEAR IT.

VISUALIZATION IS AN INCREDIBLY POWERFUL TOOL, AND ALLOWS US
TO BRING TO REALIZATION THE STUFF OF LEGEND. BOOKS THAT
CHANGE THE WORLD. GOVERNMENTS THAT BRING ABOUT WORLD
WARS. SONGS THAT BREAK HEARTS. ART THAT INSTILLS INSPIRATION
INTO PEOPLE TO CHANGE THEMSELVES.

THE MIND'S EYE IS LIKE A MUSCLE, AND BELIEVE IT OR NOT, IT IS SOME-
THING THAT ONE CAN STRENGTHEN. IT SOUNDS STRANGE, BUT IT
TRULY IS A MUSCLE THAT PERHAPS MANY OF US DO NOT EXERCISE.
THERE ARE A GREAT DEAL OF "WORKOUTS" THAT CAN BE PERFORMED
WITH VISUALIZATION, AND MANY PLACES TO FIND THESE EXERCISES.
FOR MYSELF, I FIND THAT TAKING THE TIME OUT EACH DAY TO WORK
ON THIS GENERALLY LOOKS LIKE THIS:I THINK OF A SINGLE WHEEL,
LIKE A GEAR, TURNING BY ITSELF IN BLACK SPACE. I THINK OF ITS
FORM, ITS WEIGHT, ITS SURFACE, HOW IT FEELS. THEN I ADD ANOTHER
GEAR, OF DIFFERENT SIZE, DIFFERENT COLOR, AND PLACE IT WHERE
THE FIRST GEAR TURNS IT. I CONTINUE TO DO THIS UNTIL MY
CONCENTRATION BREAKS, AND I HAVE TO START OVER.

I THINK OF A CIRCLE.
I TURN IT INTO A SPHERE.
I TURN IT INTO A SKULL.

I DO THIS WITH MANY OTHER SHAPES AND OBJECTS. WHEN I BREAK
CONCENTRATION, I BEGIN AGAIN.

I THINK OF EVENTS THAT HAVE OCCURRED, AND I EXPLORE THEM WITH ALL SENSES. I CREATE EVENTS THAT I WOULD LIKE TO HAPPEN, AND I EXPLORE THEM WITH ALL SENSES. I CREATE EVENTS THAT HAVE NOT HAPPENED, AND I PLACE THEM IN THE PAST, AS THOUGH THEY HAVE, AND I BELIEVE THAT THEY HAVE. IN THIS WAY I AM ABLE TO CHANGE REACTIONS, BREAK HABITS, SHAKE COMPULSIONS, BECAUSE I CREATE THEM SO THOROUGHLY, AND SO OFTEN, THAT THEY ARE NOT SEPARATE FROM MY MEMORY. I MAKE THEM REAL. BY CREATING OTHER SITUATIONS THAT I WOULD LIKE TO HAPPEN, I INCREASE THEIR CHANCES OF HAPPENING.

"I create events that have not happppened...and I make them real."

THE DIFFERENCE BETWEEN THIS AND "WISHFUL THINKING" IS THAT WISHFUL THINKING IS A FORM OF HOPE. I AM NOT MUCH ONE FOR HOPE. WHAT I AM DOING IS OPENING THE ROADS TO THESE SITUATIONS BY IMAGINING THEIR BEGINNINGS, WHAT STEPS LED TO THEM, HOW I CARRIED MYSELF, WHAT I DID TO ACHIEVE THEIR OCCURRENCE, AND SO ON. ESSENTIALLY, I AM PRACTICING FOR WHEN THEY DO HAPPEN, AS WELL AS DISCOVERING REALIZATIONS OF HOW TO MAKE THEM HAPPEN.

SCIENCE HAS PROVEN THAT MENTAL PRACTICE ACTUALLY MAKES US
BETTER. IT ALSO REMOVES THE FEAR OF THE UNKNOWN. IF FOR
EXAMPLE, YOU SHAKE IN YOUR BOOTS WHEN YOU THINK ABOUT
APPROACHING A WOMAN IN THE BAR, UTILIZE CREATIVE VISUALIZATION
TO BE HOW YOU WOULD LIKE YOURSELF TO BE WHEN THAT
SITUATION WAS "REAL."

ENGAGE ALL YOUR SENSES IN THE VISUALIZATION,
INCLUDING THE NERVES, THE ANXIETY, AND SO ON, AND FORCE
YOURSELF TO RELAX, TO BREAK IT, TO BE WHO YOU WOULD LIKE
YOURSELF TO BE. WITH EACH TIME YOU DO THIS, IF YOU TRULY MAKE IT
"REAL," IT WILL BECOME REAL. THESE EXPERIENCES WILL BECOME SO
LIFE-LIKE THAT THEY WILL BE ABLE TO BE BROUGHT UP FROM MEMORY,
JUST LIKE ANY "REAL" MEMORY. THEY CAN BE USED TO LEARN HOW TO
CONTROL YOUR FEAR, ANXIETY AND SO ON, BY GIVING YOU "DRY RUNS."

THIS REALLY FUCKING WORKS. GIVE IT A SHOT, AND WHEN THE
OPPORTUNITY ARISES, DON'T SABOTAGE YOURSELF BY SEPARATING
"YOUR" REALITY FROM SOME UNDERSTANDING OF
"TRUE" REALITY. THE ONLY WAY ANY HUMAN PERCEIVES THIS LIFE IS
THROUGH OUR OWN BIZARRE, SELF-CREATED CONSTRUCTS- SO MAKE
THEM WORK FOR YOU, NOT AGAINST YOU.

Who wants to be an ineffective prisoner in their own dream?

Symbolism

SYMBOLISM IS JUST A FANCY WAY OF SAYING "SHORT CUT." THAT IS EXACTLY
WHAT WE ARE DOING WHEN WE ENGAGE IN SIGIL WORK, OR ANY OTHER
FORM OF WRITTEN ANYTHING, REALLY. A WORD IS JUST A SHORT CUT TO A
LARGER IDEA THAT I WOULD HAVE TO SHOW YOU. ALL LANGUAGE IS SYM-
BOLISM. I CAN SAY "BEAR" I CAN MAKE THAT VIBRATION WITH MY THROAT,
AND ANYONE WHO SPEAKS THIS LANGUAGE OF SYMBOLS, WHO IS FAMILIAR
WITH THIS UTTERLY COMPLEX SYSTEM, KNOWS ESSENTIALLY WHAT I MEAN,
WITHOUT ME HAVING TO GRUNT, TAKE THEM BY THE ARM, AND WALK
OUT INTO THE WOODS TO FIND A GRIZZLY.

IT'S THE SAME WITH MAGICAL
SYMBOLISM (AND I OF COURSE,
WOULD ARGUE THAT LANGUAGE IS
MAGIC OF A HIGH DEGREE;
ANOTHER "LEARNABLE SYSTEM"
THAT CONTINUOUSLY CHANGES
REALITY THROUGH DIFFERENT
VIBRATORY PATTERNS- WE'LL GET
TO THAT NEXT). WHAT WE ARE
DOING IS TAKING A VERY
COMPLICATED (OR SOMETIMES
VERY SIMPLE) IDEA, AND CREATING
A SHORT-HAND IMAGE FOR IT
THAT COMMUNICATES TO US THE
VERY "THING-NESS" OF THAT IDEA
WHEN WE LOOK AT IT, A SYMBOL
THAT CONJURES UP ALL OF OUR
EMOTION AND FEELING AND
UNDERSTANDING OF THAT ONE
IDEA IT IS MEANT TO EXPRESS.

THIS IS ONE REASON WHY I DO NOT PARTICULARLY
CARE FOR THE COMMON FORMS OF SIGIL WORK
FOUND IN CHAOS-MAGICIANS LIKE AUSTIN OSMAN
SPARE'S WORK (STILL A FASCINATING READ ON "CHAOS
MAGIC" THAT ONE CAN GET A LOT OUT OF. HIS WRIT-
INGS, ALONG WITH PETER CARROLL'S "LIBER NULL," AND
"PSYCHONAUT" ARE CLASSICS OF THE GENRE). IT IS, IN
MY OPINION, TOO RAPID, TOO SLOPPY, TOO "EASY."
HOW CAN WE CREATE A SYMBOL POWERFUL ENOUGH
TO ENCAPSULATE EVEN OUR IDEA AND EXPERIENCE
WITH THE WORD "TOMATO" BY SIMPLY TAKING OUT
THE VOWELS OF THE WORD, AND SLAPPING THE
CONSONANTS TOGETHER IN A WAY THAT
"LOOKS COOL?"

HELL, EVEN A TOMATO HAS BEEN EXPERIENCED IN SOME FORM
OR ANOTHER THROUGHOUT MOST OF OUR LIVES. ITS SMELL,
TASTE, TOUCH, LOOK- OUR RELATIONSHIP WITH IT, PERHAPS
DISGUST, OR COMFORT, OR THAT IT REMINDS US OF OUR
MOTHER IN THE GARDEN IN THE SUMMERTIME. NOTHING IS
TRULY SIMPLE, AT THE END OF THE DAY.

WE HAVE TO GO DEEPER IF WE ARE TO MAKE A SIGIL THAT
ACTUALLY HAS POWER, AND WE DO THIS THROUGH THE
UNDERSTANDING THAT THE SIGIL ITSELF HAS NO POWER.
EVERY TIME I HEAR SOME CHARLATAN TALK ABOUT HOW PEOPLE
SHOULDN'T GET THIS RUNE OR THAT RUNE TATTOOED ON
THEM, OR BE CAREFUL WITH USING THIS SYMBOL OR THAT, IT
BRINGS UP BILE IN THE BACK OF MY THROAT.

NONSENSE. THEY ARE GODDAMN LINES. WHAT MAKES THEM POWERFUL, THE ONLY THING THAT MAKES THEM POWERFUL, IS OURSELVES, OUR RELATIONSHIP TO THEM. WHAT FEELINGS AND IDEAS AND PASSIONS THEY AWAKEN IN US, THEY DO SO BECAUSE WE HAVE CREATED THEM WITH THAT ABILITY. WE HAVE PROVIDED THESE OBJECTS WITH A FATE, A DOOM. WE ARE THE DEMIURGE OF THE UNIVERSE THAT ENCAPSULATES THAT ONE SYMBOL. THEY EXIST TO DO WHAT WE MADE THEM TO DO.

"We are the demiurge of the universe that encapsulates that one symbol..."

SO, TO CREATE AN EFFECTIVE SIGIL, IS TO PLUMB THE DEPTHS OF YOURSELF, YOUR CONSCIOUS AND SUBCONSCIOUS, TO UTTERLY DELVE INTO WHAT MAKES THIS THING CONNECT WITH YOU IN YOUR PERCEPTION OF REALITY, ON ALL LEVELS, AND THEN TO CREATE A SYMBOL THAT JOGS THAT MASSIVE COLLECTION OF IDEAS.

EVER SEEN A PICTURE OF A CARBURETOR IN ONE OF THOSE MECHANIC MANUALS, THEY CALL IT "EXPLODED VIEW", WHERE YOU CAN SEE EVERY LITTLE PART SEPARATED OUT BY LINES? THAT'S WHAT YOU'RE DOING WITH A SIGIL. TAKING ALL THESE LITTLE TINY PARTS, AND CREATING A MASSIVE, FUNCTIONAL WHOLE OUT OF THEM, AND KNOWING IT INSIDE AND OUT, SO THAT WHEN YOU SEE THE SIGIL, IT EXPLODES INTO ALL ITS MINUTE AND FASCINATING PARTS. THE ULTIMATE SHORTCUT TO A FEELING, A PRINCIPLE, AN IDEA, OR WHATEVER.

THE SAME GOES FOR CREATING OBJECTS, AND JESUS, I'M
ABOUT TO SAY THIS- "MAGICAL ITEMS." TRUST ME, I KNOW
HOW THIS SOUNDS. BEAR WITH ME... YOU'LL TOTALLY
LEVEL UP.

IMAGINE FOR A SECOND THAT I CREATE A SYMBOL, USING
THE LAST PART OF THIS DISCUSSION TO COMPLETELY EN-
CAPSULATE THE IDEA OF "PHYSICAL STRENGTH/POWER," SO
STRONGLY THAT WHEN I SEE IT, IT LITERALLY MAKES ME SEE
RED, CALLS UP A ROARING SAVAGE FROM DEEP WITHIN ME
AND GETS ME PSYCHED UP LIKE A BERSERKER ON COCAINE.
WHAT I DO NEXT IS CREATE A PHYSICAL OBJECT THAT
MAKES SENSE TO MARRY THAT SYMBOL TO, SO THAT IT
GAINS STRENGTH THROUGH THE CREATION OF A PROCESS
CALLED "LAYERING." LIKE, HOW A JOKE IS FUNNIER IF IT
WORKS ON A LOT OF LEVELS AT ONCE-
THAT SORT OF THING.

SO I TAKE MY SIGIL, AND PUT IT ON A CHALK
BAG THAT I USE WHEN I DEADLIFT. I KEEP IT
SEPARATE FROM MY OTHER CHALK, BECAUSE I
ONLY USE THIS WHEN ATTEMPTING A PERSON-
AL RECORD. THAT MAKES IT SPECIAL, GIVES IT
MORE POWER AS I CREATE A DISTINCTION BE-
TWEEN IT AND MY "NORMAL" CHALK. THEN I
GO A STEP FURTHER- I MARK IT ON THE BAG
WITH PAINT MADE FROM OBJECTS THAT ARE
CONSONANT WITH THAT IDEA. I THINK OF
WHAT ANIMALS REPRESENT THIS CONCEPT,
AND I USE THEIR BLOOD, OR THEIR BONES IN
THE PAINT. I USE A LIQUID TESTOSTERONE
PRODUCT IN IT. I COMBINE PLANT ELEMENTS
AND SO ON, ALL THAT HOLD A SPECIAL PLACE
OF MEANING FOR ME, AND THE OUTCOME OF
THIS IS A PHYSICAL OBJECT THAT IS CAPABLE OF
CHANGING MY MINDSET.

IT ALTERS REALITY FOR ME IN A VERY REAL WAY. WHEN I USE THAT
CHALK, I FUCK SHIT UP. I LOSE MY MIND IN THE ACT OF SAVAGELY
MOVING HEAVY SHIT. IT MOVES ME FROM A NORMAL MAN INTO AN
ANIMAL. AND JUST LIKE VISUALIZATION...IT REALLY, REALLY WORKS.
GO TRY IT.

Vocalization

MOST OF THE WORDS THAT WE WILL SPEAK IN OUR LIFE ARE INCANTATIONS, BECAUSE MOST WORDS ARE SPOKEN TO ELICIT SOME SORT OF OCCURRENCE, CHANGE, ACTION, ETC IN THOSE WHO HEAR THEM. LIKE ANY OF THE OTHER STUFF WE'VE DISCUSSED SO FAR, THERE IS A WAY TO PRACTICE THE USE OF WORDS IN ORDER TO MAKE THEM MORE EFFECTIVE, WHETHER WRITTEN (SIGIL-WORK) OR SPOKEN (VOCALIZATION.)

THE SAME RULES APPLY HERE AS ELSEWHERE. YOUR WORDS, IF POWERFUL, CREATE CHANGE. WITHOUT A THOROUGH UNDERSTANDING OF OUR GOALS, OR WHAT WE ARE TRYING TO ACHIEVE, THESE CHANGES THEY CREATE WILL BE SCATTERED, WEAK, INEFFECTUAL, LACKING MOMENTUM OR WEIGHT. A STRONG SPEAKER WAS GENERALLY NOT BORN THAT WAY- THEY CREATED THEMSELVES TO BE THAT, BY DOING THAT.

"Your words, if powerful, create change."

AT THIS POINT, I WILL SOUND LIKE A SELF-HELP GURU, BUT WHEN I WAS A YOUNG TEENAGER, I WAS, LIKE A LOT OF OTHER TEENAGERS, EXTREMELY SHY. I HAD THREE OLDER BROTHERS WHO HAD MADE ALL MY FRIENDS FOR ME, AND I WAS VERY UNCOMFORTABLE START- ING CONVERSATIONS OR APPROACHING PEOPLE I DIDN'T KNOW. AT AROUND 14, I MOVED WITH MY PARENTS, AND COULD NO LONGER RELY ON MY BROTHERS' CHARISMA TO MAKE MY CONNECTIONS. THE REALIZATION OF THIS DROVE ME TO FORCE MYSELF INTO SITU- ATIONS WHERE I WOULD HAVE TO COMMUNICATE, ENGAGE WITH OTHER PEOPLE, USE MY SPEECH AND PRESENCE TO GET THE THINGS I NEEDED OUT OF LIFE.

ONE OF THE WAYS I DID THIS WAS BY CREATING VOCALIZED CUES FOR MYSELF EACH MORNING, WHICH IS A LESS FEEBLE WAY OF SAYING "DAILY AFFIRMATIONS," EVEN THOUGH THAT'S WHAT IT WAS. I PINPOINTED THINGS ABOUT MYSELF THAT I WANTED TO CHANGE, THAT I DID NOT LIKE ABOUT MYSELF, OR THINGS THAT I DID LIKE, BUT WANTED TO STRENGTHEN, AND I VOCALIZED THOSE THINGS.

THE WAY THAT I DID THIS CAN BE UTILIZED BY ANYONE. IT IS AN ADDITION/SUBTRACTION THING, AND IS LARGELY BASED ON FIRST DEEPENING YOUR SELF-KNOWLEDGE THROUGH HAVING NO MERCY FOR YOURSELF. WE DON'T OFTEN LIKE TO POINT OUT IN OURSELVES OR ADMIT THE THINGS THAT WE ARE WEAK AT OR DON'T LIKE. I DON'T MEAN GENTLE THINGS LIKE "I AM A LITTLE HEAVY," OR "I AVOID CONFRONTA-TION," BUT "I EXHIBIT SIGNS OF EX-TREME LAZINESS AND LACK OF SELF CONTROL," OR, "I HAVE DISPLAYED COWARDLY BEHAVIOR IN THE PAST." THESE ARE THE HARDER EDGES OF THOSE SOFT HALF TRUTHS.

NOTICE THE LANGUAGE I USED, HOWEVER, WHEN POINTING OUT THE FAILINGS: I DID NOT SAY "I AM LAZY," OR "I AM A COWARD." LIKE MOST THINGS, THE WAY THAT WE VOCALIZE IS OFTEN MORE IMPOR-TANT THAN THE WHAT. BY SAYING "I AM THIS OR I AM THAT," WE CREATE A PATHWAY IN OUR BRAIN. WE AFFIRM THAT WE ARE THAT THING THAT WE DESPISE. WE SET OURSELVES UP TO BELIEVE THAT, BY WORDING IT THAT WAY. SINCE OUR WORDS ARE POWERFUL, WE IN-STEAD VOCALIZE INCANTATIONS OF CHANGE- "I AM NOT WHO I WAS, AND I AM NOT BOUND BY WHAT I HAVE BEEN. I AM ONLY WHAT I AM BECOMING, AT THIS TIME, AND IN THIS MOMENT, I AM BECOMING STRONGER. I AM BECOMING MORE BRAVE. I AM EVERY DAY BECOMING MORE THAN I WAS."

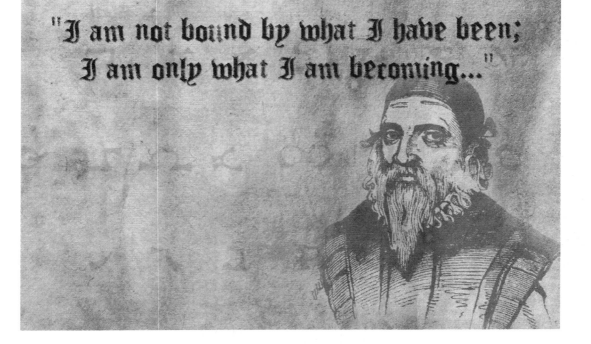

"I am not bound by what I have been;
I am only what I am becoming..."

THESE LINES OF THOUGHT
CREATE THEIR OWN PATH-
WAYS IN THE BRAIN. THEY
STRENGTHEN POSITIVE PAT-
TERNS OF THINKING, AND BY
VOCALIZATION, WE BRING
THEM FROM THE SHADOWY
REALMS OF THOUGHT AND
DREAM INTO REALITY. A
THING, ONCE SPOKEN, BE-
COMES MORE TRUE. THE
MORE IT IS SPOKEN, THE
TRUER IT BECOMES, THE
MORE WE BELIEVE IT. YOU'VE
HEARD THE SAYING "FAKE IT
'TIL YOU MAKE IT?"

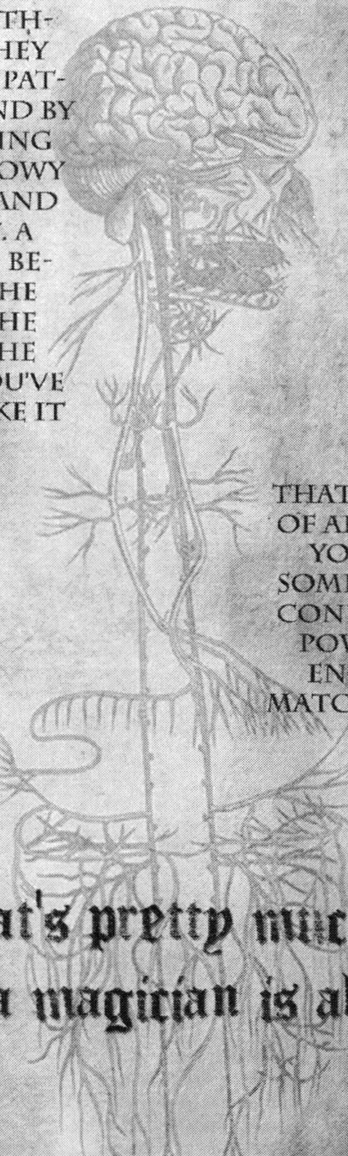

THAT IS A NO-BULLSHIT PIECE
OF ADVICE. IT DOESN'T MAKE
YOU FAKE. IT MAKES YOU
SOMEONE WHO IS UTILIZING
CONFIDENCE AND PERSONAL
POWER IN LIEU OF EXPERI-
ENCE, UNTIL HIS REALITY
MATCHES HIS VIEW OF HOW IT
SHOULD BE-

...and that's pretty much what being
a magician is about.

ANOTHER FORM OF PRACTICING EMPOWERING YOUR WORDS IS THROUGH RITUAL. AND EVEN THOUGH WE'VE SORT OF BRIEFLY DIS- CUSSED IT, I WANT TO EXPAND FIRST ON THE THE IDEA THAT BREAKING DOWN THE BARRIERS BETWEEN "RITUAL" AND THE REST OF YOUR LIFE, THROUGH THE CONSTANT PRACTICE OF RITUAL THINKING AND RITUAL ACTION IS WHAT WE ARE SEEKING TO ACCOMPLISH AS MAGICIANS. WHAT WE ARE LOOKING TO DO IS MAKE THE WHOLE OF OUR LIVES INTO ONE GREAT BIG MYTHOLOGICAL RE-TELLING, WITH YOU AS THE CENTRAL ROLE.

THE WAY THAT WE DO THIS IS BY LENDING WEIGHT TO EACH WORD AND ACTION THROUGH RITUAL THINKING. WHAT I MEAN WHEN I SAY RITUAL THINKING IS A SORT OF CONSTANT AWARENESS THAT WE ARE, WITH EVERY MOMENT OF OUR LIVES, TELLING A STORY, "CASTING A SPELL," IF YOU WILL, FOR BETTER OR WORSE, FOR CREATION OR DESTRUCTION, FOR HEROISM OR VILLAINY. WHAT DO WE WANT THAT STORY TO READ LIKE, A THOU- SAND YEARS FROM NOW? IF WE THINK THIS WAY, WE WILL CHOOSE OUR WORDS MORE CAREFULLY, MORE STRONGLY. WE WILL ENSURE THAT THEY ARE BACKED BY ACTION.

"𝕎ith every moment of our lives, we are casting a spell for better or worse."

IN THIS MANNER, WE WILL AWAKEN IN THE MORNING WITH THE KNOWLEDGE THAT TODAY WE WILL SHAPE OUR LEGEND. OUR MORN- ING WORK OUT TAKES ON A GREATER IMPORT, WHEN WE DO IT WITH THE INTENT OF BECOMING STRONGER TO BE BETTER ABLE TO TELL THE KIND OF STORY WE WANT. IT IS A RITUAL OF STRENGTH.

WHEN WE EAT, WE ARE DOING SO WITH THE INTENT OF FUELING THE MACHINE THAT IS OUR BODY AND MIND, AND WE WILL MAKE BETTER CHOICES OF WHAT WE PUT INTO IT IF WE THINK THIS WAY.

WHEN WE SPEAK, OUR WORDS WILL SPIRAL OUTWARD FROM US AS WE INVOKE GREATNESS. WE WILL TAKE CARE NOT TO WASTE TOO MUCH TIME IN IDLE OR VAIN CHATTER. WE WILL ENSURE THAT WHAT WE SPEAK INTO EXISTENCE IS FITTING FOR OUR GREATER NARRATIVE, OUR LIVING MYTH.

THIS IS THE META-RITUAL, THE OVER-
ARCHING GREAT WORK THAT WILL
TAKE OUR ENTIRE LIVES TO ACCOM-
PLISH (OR PERHAPS LONGER). BUT WE
CAN ALSO PERFORM MICRORITUALS,
WHICH ARE, IN ESSENCE, SMALL REPRE-
SENTATIONS OF THE WHOLE OF THE
GREAT WORK, AND ARE THEMSELVES A
RE-TELLING OF THE GREAT CREATION
MYTHS. WE BECOME THE WORD, OR
YMIR, "THE ROARING", OUR VIBRA-
TIONS COALESCING TO BECOME PO-
TENTIAL, OUR MINDS, WILLS, AND EC-
STATIC VISION THE TOOLS WE USE TO
SHAPE OUR REALITY ANEW BY SPEAKING
IT INTO EXISTENCE!

THE SUCCESSFUL WRITING OF RITUAL CAN TAKE MANY FORMS,
AND THERE ARE REALLY NO RULES TO CONDUCTING THEM. THEY
CAN BE AS SIMPLE AS A BASIC PRAYER UPON RISING, OR AS COMPLEX
AS ANY CEREMONY FROM AN OLD GRIMOIRE- THE QUESTION IS:
WHAT DO YOU NEED IN ORDER TO MAKE THE RITUAL A FULFILL-
ING AND, MORE IMPORTANTLY, FUNCTIONAL EXPERIENCE. RITUAL
IS USED, ABOVE ALL, TO RE-EMPHASIZE YOUR GREATER NARRATIVE,
TO REMIND YOU OF YOUR PURPOSE AND TO RECHARGE YOU FOR
THE TASK AT HAND. AGAIN, THERE ARE NO HARD AND FAST "RULES"
BUT SINCE SOME GUIDELINES CAN OFTEN HELP, HERE ARE SOME I
USE:

- KNOWING WHAT WE ARE TRYING TO ACCOMPLISH. THIS GOES BACK TO HAVING A GOAL. WE DON'T WANT TO SPEND ENERGY IN RANDOM DIRECTIONS, OR WE WILL ACHIEVE NO DEFINED RESULT. LIKE I SAID ABOVE, THIS CAN BE A LOT OF THINGS, BUT MY USUAL RITUALS ARE TO RE-CHARGE MYSELF, AND TO REMIND MYSELF THAT I AM LIVING MYTH, OUTSIDE OF ANY LINEAR CONCEPT OF SPACE AND TIME, RE-TELLING THE STORIES OF THE GODS AND CREATION WITH MY VERY LIFE. BIG IDEAS REQUIRE BIG EXECUTION, BUT THIS DOESN'T HAVE TO MEAN BOMBASTIC OR RIDICULOUS. FIND A REASON, KNOW YOUR WILL. EXECUTE IT STRONGLY.

- ENGAGING ALL THE SENSES. LIKE WE DID WITH CREATIVE VISUALIZA-TION, WE WANT TO INCLUDE THE ENTIRE RANGE OF SENSORY EXPERI-ENCE INTO OUR RITUAL. WE DO THIS BY AGAIN USING CREATIVE VISUALIZATION TO ACCOMPLISH THAT. THE WAY OUR RITUAL SPACE LOOKS WILL GO A LONG WAY TOWARD PUTTING US IN THE RIGHT HEADSPACE TO CONDUCT IT-

AGAIN, THIS IS ENTIRELY PERSONAL AND BASED AROUND WHAT WORKS FOR YOU. A BONFIRE BLAZING UNDER THE FULLMOON WITH BLOOD ON YOUR FACE, OR A QUIET CHAMBER OF REFLECTION. THIS IS YOUR STORY, NOT ANYONE ELSE'S.

THE SOUNDS OF WIND AND WATER, CALMING CHIMES OR RABID BLACK METAL. THE SMELL OF INCENSE BURNING ON THE ALTAR, OR OF LIQUOR SPRAYED OVER BLEACHED BONES.

THE FLAVOR OF TOBACCO OFFERED TO THE SPIRITS OF THE LAND, OR THE TASTE OF GRAVEYARD EARTH UNDER THE TONGUE AS IT SPEAKS WITH THE DEAD.

THE FEEL OF THE RITUAL KNIFE, COMFORTING AND FAMILIAR IN THE PALM, THE WATERSNAKE OF FEAR RISING UP FROM THE GUTS AS THE PLANT ALLIES TAKE HOLD, OR THE MAD ECSTASY OF FLESH ON FLESH TO HEIGHTEN THE CONSCIOUSNESS OR LOWER IT THROUGH THE SEXUAL ACT. DECIDE WHAT YOU WILL USE TO ALTER YOUR CONSCIOUSNESS, AND CREATE WITH IT.

- SPEAKING YOUR WILL INTO EXISTENCE. WHAT WE ARE DOING WITH RITUAL IS RE-MAKING THE FUCKING WORLD AS WE SEE FIT.

THIS IS A HEAVY SACRAMENT TO PARTAKE IN, AND A GLORIOUS ONE. SPEAK YOUR WORDS INTO THE WELL OF WYRD, LAYERING IT INTO THE STRATA OF REALITY, KNOWING THAT AS YOU SPEAK, THE WORLD AROUND YOU CHANGES. BELIEVE IN YOURSELF AND YOUR ABILITY TO CATALYZE MASSIVE HAPPENINGS
WITH NOTHING MORE
THAN A
WORD.

UNDERSTAND THAT SPEECH IS A GOD-LIKE GIFT, AND USE IT
ACCORDINGLY.

PERFORM YOUR RITUALS WITH CERTAINTY
AND PERFORM THEM OFTEN.

GRADUALLY THE LINES WILL BLUR, THE VEILS WILL PART AND THE BRIDE WHO HIDES BEHIND THEM WILL MAKE HERSELF KNOWN.

HER NAME IS POWER, AND SHE WAITS FOR YOU TO COME TAKE HER.

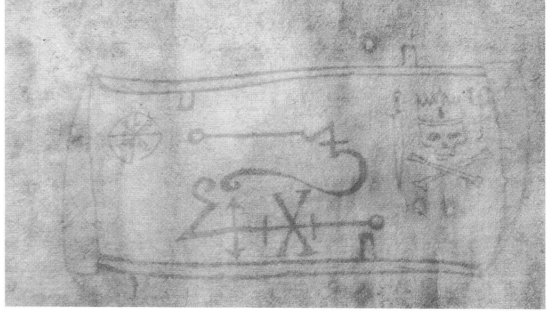

THESE THINGS REALLY ARE THE BASIC FRAMEWORK OF EVERY SYSTEM OF MAGIC, AND I BELIEVE IN THEIR USE AS INCREDIBLY POWERFUL TOOLS OF SELF-CREATION, AND ACTUALIZATION.

I ALSO BELIEVE THAT WE HAVE TO TAKE THINGS ONE STEP AT A TIME. YOU CAN'T WALK INTO A GYM AS A 120 POUND WEAKLING AND THROW THREE HUNDRED POUNDS ON THE BAR AND BENCH IT. IT WILL FUCKING CRUSH YOU. THIS SORTA THING IS THE SAME WAY.

ONLY AN IDIOT COMES AT THIS WITH THE EXPECTATION OF SUCCESS WITHOUT WORK. THOSE WHO ARE DIRECTED AND GROUNDED WILL REALIZE THAT THE BASE MUST BE STRONG FOR ANYTHING OF WORTH TO BE BUILT ON IT. START SIMPLE, START SLOW, START BASIC, BUT BY ALL MEANS, START.

MAKE IT WORK FOR YOU THROUGH CONSISTENT APPLICATION OF THE TOOLS, THROUGH THE DISCOVERY OF NEW TOOLS, THROUGH THE UNDERSTANDING OF THE BEST WAY TO APPLY THEM.

I HOPE THIS HELPS IN SOME WAY TO CREATE OR INSPIRE A NEW BREED OF MAGICIAN WHO TAKES A NO BULLSHIT APPROACH, WITH THE UNDERSTANDING THAT THIS STUFF REALLY DOES WORK-

BUT ONLY IF YOU DO.

- Paul Waggener,

Halloween, MMXV

PAUL WAGGENER

WWW.OPERATIONWEREWOLF.COM

72916001R00108

Made in the USA
Lexington, KY
05 December 2017